This Place is a Zoo!

This Place is a Zoo!

How to Manage the Unmanageable Organization

Michael D. LaRue

Writer's Showcase
San Jose New York Lincoln Shanghai

This Place is a Zoo!
How to Manage the Unmanageable Organization

Writer's Showcase
an imprint of iUniverse, Inc.

For information address:
iUniverse, Inc.
5220 S. 16th St., Suite 200
Lincoln, NE 68512
www.iuniverse.com

ISBN: 0-595-23498-4

Printed in the United States of America

Contents

Acknowledgements

I always wished I could write with no errors. Word Processing helps but still those errors creep in. Nancy Cherry has edited my writings for many years and stepped up to the plate once again, not only to edit the text of this book, but also to offer many constructive comments. What I write is always made better by her diligence.

Gary Clarke continues to provide me with good advice. I worked for him for many years at the Topeka Zoo and learned a great deal about management. He was gracious enough to review this book and offer his expertise.

Ron Kaufman and I worked a number of years together at the Topeka Zoo. He is an excellent writer and wrote the original draft of the animal standards of care for the Topeka Zoo. The final document is much changed but probably would not have existed at all without his knowledge and attention to detail.

I was fortunate that many people I worked for over the years allowed me to attend training and planning meetings that helped shape my views. Some of the same people gave me the freedom to try many of my ideas. Some did not.

So many of my thoughts and views about management were filtered through Lanette Scurlock who was always good enough to tell me how crazy my ideas were or point out good reasons why they wouldn't work. I always knew that if she thought they were reasonable, they would work. Roger Scurlock took the photo appearing in this book.

Finally, Jan Conley hired me when I made a major career change and provided me with much information about being a good manager. Even though I was in the lowest position in the organizational structure, she always made me feel important and a vital part of the organization. That is a good manager!

Introduction

"This place is a zoo!" is usually exclaimed to describe something in chaos, disorganized, unmanageable or even a real Zoo. To keep the two "zoos" straight, the lower case zoo means, "This place is a zoo!" The upper case Zoo means a real Zoo. This is an important distinction because most of my career was spent working in a Zoo that was often a zoo.

Most organizations have a governing authority. The type of governing authority often is a clue about whether the organization is an unmanageable one or a manageable one. Unmanageable organizations have governing authorities made up of elected officials, councils/commissions or quasi government boards. Unfortunately, this type of governing authority dooms the best-intentioned management. Government governing authorities are by far the most difficult in which to manage an organization.

This work will explore why this is so and present possibilities for attempting to manage unmanageable organizations. Many of the possibilities are based on aspects of strategic planning, recent management theory and my nearly 30 years of experience working in a Zoological Park with a government governing authority. Since my experience is in a Zoo, many of the examples used come from that Zoo work. However, these examples are easily transferred to any organization with a difficult governing authority.

For those who have tried to manage an unmanageable organization and either failed or are struggling, take heart. Managing an unmanageable organization has little to do with skill, with management ability or with any knowledge you may have. You need those things but success can be more a matter of having a decent governing authority and no influential enemies. It's a matter of survival and whether the good out-balances the bad.

Finding a career that you are passionate about is very rewarding. It is unfortunate that many of those careers are tied up in government governing authorities that do their best to quell the passion and sometimes terminate careers. It is a risk that is both rewarding and discouraging.

This books assumes that you are a good manager, interested in innovation, in success and in seeing your organization be the best.

It is my hope that by reading this, you will gain some skills, enhance your management ability and add to your knowledge. At the least, I hope you will better understand why your organization seems unmanageable and why it is unmanageable. At the most, I hope you can use this information to not only survive but also manage your unmanageable organization for as long as you wish with a minimum of stress.

Chapter 1

It All Happened in Peculiar

It all happened in Peculiar, a midwestern town on the smallish side. The town wasn't really known for much but the town employed Bob for most of his adult life. He worked at the Peculiar Public Gardens (PPG but they didn't make paint). PPG was a public attraction, a popular one, which exhibited things. People came from miles around to marvel at the unique attractions that PPG provided the community.

Bob used to work there but no longer does. It wasn't that he wanted to leave. After all, he had studied for this job in college, worked his up from the lowest position to the highest, learned from some of the best in the business and passed up other opportunities so that one day he might be The Director. At the peak of his career, doing what he loved to do, word came about a change at PPG and there would be a new Director. No warning. In a matter of hours, he was packing boxes alone while his senior staff was meeting behind closed doors discussing things (he was cut off from these things too).

PPG is mostly tax supported but did receive 30% to 50% of its operating revenue from other sources, mainly gate receipts but also State appropriations and private donations. PPG is part of the town's Park Department whose director reports to a Chief Operating Officer who reports to the Mayor who is elected to run the town. There is also a town council make up of elected representatives who set policy for the town. PPG also has a support group, The Friends of PPG or FOPPG.

FOPPG has an interesting arrangement with PPG and the town. They sell memberships. Through town council policy, members of FOPPG are admitted free to PPG. In addition, PPG gives FOPPG office space, utilities and some PPG staff time so that FOPPG can process and collect membership fees so members can enter PPG without paying a gate fee (PPG revenue). In exchange, PPG received from FOPPG certain things that were of benefit to PPG. Bob admitted to me that he could not really remember what benefits had much value to PPG but he did recall the cost/benefit analysis he compiled was not well received.

Bob also admitted that it was very difficult to get funds from FOPPG for projects or programs. This was money that PPG would have received as gate revenue but instead got stuck in FOPPG.

The day Bob received a call from the Mayor informing him of his promotion to Director of PPG, was one of his happiest days. It didn't occur to him until later that the Mayor was two layers of bureaucracy away and shouldn't the Park Director have promoted him? He didn't think about it much since he had the job he had dreamed of.

The first couple of years seemed uneventful. Bob worked at getting some new attractions because they are necessary to keep the public coming and paying a fee. It occurred to him that not only is a new attraction important but the Gardens should be open when the majority of people have time to come. So, why not be open in the evenings and on holidays. He already knew that the majority of people visited on weekends when they are not working. It all made sense to him.

The staff did not accept this logic. They wanted to work 8:00 am to 5:00 pm. Some suggested the Gardens close on weekends and holidays so they could be off. Bob wondered why the staff wasn't interested in maximizing public visitation and revenue, as was he.

Then there was the new exhibit. It was a totally new concept that attracted a number of private donations. FOPPG was in charge of collecting these donations. The first donation was a good one but not all that large. FOPPG told the donor they could put their name on the exhibit. Suddenly, there weren't many more large gifts.

The staff was again upset. They wanted to know why the money wasn't being used to upgrade existing facilities. They also wanted to know why so much money had already been spent on public facilities like rest rooms and a concessions area near the new exhibit. And, they wanted a raise.

PPG needed this new exhibit and it was finally completed. At the grand opening, a visitor walked through an open service gate and tripped over a box breaking his leg. The visitor sued the town. The supervisor of the exhibit filed a disciplinary action against the employee for leaving the service gate open. The employee filed a grievance against just about everyone charging that he was inadequately trained, he had not been specifically told to close the service gate on this particular day at this particular time, the supervisor was not qualified and PPG was mismanaged.

The grievance was considered by a long time Peculiar employee in the Personnel Department who decided that with so many complaints, one or more of them had to be true. She notified the town's Legal Department that PPG should be investigated.

A few days after the broken leg incident, Bob received a call from a TV station wanting to interview him about the new exhibit. This would be a good way to get some positive news out to the public, Bob thought. At the interview, the first question was, "A few days ago a visitor broke his leg in the new exhibit, so is it true the Gardens are unsafe for visitors?"

Bob then got a call from a Federal government official representing one of the agencies that licenses PPG to operate. She told him that they had received a complaint that PPG was not providing adequate training for its employees and was generally mismanaged. They must investigate every complaint even though the complainant was anonymous. They would be sending an investigator.

One of the Board members of FOPPG was also a State Legislator. He announced at a FOPPG board meeting that since it appeared the

Gardens were mismanaged, based on all the news reports, he was recommending the State appropriation to support PPG be eliminated. The Board, believing the Legislator to be a powerful person, didn't see anything wrong with this idea. They then voted to fund a membership drive to sell more memberships.

The Federal investigator reported that employees at PPG were not adequately trained. Although neither the investigator, nor anyone in the Federal agency could define "adequately trained", they all felt it must be true because an employee did not close a service gate resulting in an injury.

There were letters to the editor and news stories every day. Bob was asked to write volumes to explain why employees had to work on weekends, why he wanted a contract with FOPPG and why the sky was blue on some days.

At the end of his employment with PPG, Bob finally realized that he had been trying to manage an unmanageable organization. With all the clues he had, Bob had missed this fact.

The scenario just presented has happened all or in part in many organizations. It is a combination of situations faced by friends around the country who have tried to manage unmanageable organizations. Some have failed. Some are still trying and are under tremendous stress. A few have succeeded (the last I heard, anyway).

As difficult as it seems to be to manage an unmanageable organization, there are some skills and techniques that can help. That's what follows in this book. I wish I had read this book before I tried to manage an unmanageable organization and I know Bob would wish the same thing. No matter what job you have in an unmanageable organization, everyone needs to know how to deal with the press, with antagonists, with staff, with support organizations, with governing authorities, with donors, with government oversight organizations and have a plan and a strategy for working that ensures the organization's success and keeps you employed.

The real key to managing an unmanageable organization is bringing together "publics" that have an interest in the organization and putting together a plan for today and for the future. We will get to that later. First, there are a few primary things you need to know so you can deal with them from the day you start the job. After all, planning takes time. But today, the press is calling for an interview.

It's too late for Bob but for you, let's get started.

Chapter 2

The Press

You just received that promotion or were just hired as the manager of an unmanageable organization. You have not had time to hold your first staff meeting and the press is calling to schedule an interview with you. You need to quickly know how to handle the press so you can start your new job on a positive note.

Unmanageable organizations are usually public organizations and subject to public scrutiny. The press is a component of this public scrutiny and often plays a pivotal role in how the public perceives your organization. A good manager has to recognize this fact and learn to deal with the press in a way that creates a positive image for your organization. Not an easy task.

The press has a different agenda than your organization. First and foremost to the press is drawing readers or viewers or listeners so that more advertising can be sold or more subscriptions can be sold. There is usually a code of ethics that journalists follow but it would be a mistake on your part to rely on that possibility as you deal with the press. The press will pursue any report that will generate news and your views as to whether it is news or not doesn't matter.

There are many ways the press can get information about your organization that they may or may not use. Your organization may push news through press releases. It is actually a good idea for you to do so. You should not only release news that is always good and complimentary but also news, that if released by someone else or "found out," could be perceived another way. It's a mistake to flood the press with news releases. It is also a mistake to withhold potential news items. There is a balance with no clear formula. Consider the release of information carefully and ensure it creates both trust and openness with the press.

Press releases must be well written. If you write press releases, have a professional look them over to ensure that are written clearly and provide the information you want to convey. The best approach is to have a staff person who is trained in working with the press and can write well do all press releases. You may not feel you have as much control but a poorly written press release can put you in a position you do not wish to be. You may spend many long hours trying to explain something gleaned from a bad press release that was simply a mistake in writing or a mistake in the way the information was presented.

In our society, anyone with a different view or opinion may choose to express that view or opinion with the press. It may become news that could put you, as the manager, in a defensive position especially if the view or opinion is a negative one about the organization or even you. In reality the news has been made. Your response and how you respond simply make the news harder or softer. Understand that the techniques used for responding are different for newspaper, radio and television. However, there are a few things common for each of these that you follow:

- Be calm
- Be confident
- Be honest
- "No comment" is a no-no

If you get a call from a newspaper reporter for comments on a news story, invite them to visit you at your organization. You will feel more comfortable on your turf. In addition, you then have the advantage of using your personality and your location to provide unspoken, positive elements that may make bad news not so bad and good news better. Answer each question carefully, directly and honestly. Newspaper is the one type of media that can give you room to explain things in some detail. Use it wisely. Understand that the reporter needs to write a story that is factual and will capture the interest of the paper's readers. Keep to the point but use the opportunity to embellish with interesting facts. You might change the story from one that started out as a negative one to one that is positive.

If you get a call from a radio newsperson for comments on a news story, take a deep breath. Radio and television both operate on sound bites. These are pieces of information that are only a few seconds long. You must learn to give factual, honest answers in sound bites. Time is a precious commodity in the airways and long comments cannot be used. Give the facts in 5 seconds if possible. You'll get your whole sentence out and, if there is time, maybe a second sentence. Radio news usually records your phone conversation later editing what was said by cutting out most of what you said. The whole conversation will not likely be aired. Don't ramble and don't constantly repeat yourself. The radio interview is the most difficult and the most dangerous in that you have so little control over what the outcome will be. You don't have the luxury of seeing the person interviewing you thus miss a lot of visual cues like their facial expression in reaction to something you said. You don't get to size up the situation, the location or any other people's presence.

If you get a call from a television reporter for comments on a news story, they will likely want to visit you with a camera and reporter. Not only do you need to answer questions in sound bites but you also must be able to present yourself in a calm and confident manner in front of the camera. It is not just your verbal reaction that will be captured but your visual presentation (body language) will also be captured. Your frowns and smiles and confusion, all will be there. That means you must learn to control your visual self. Reporters like to ask questions that will create strong emotion in the person being interviewed. Notice that when a question is asked to someone and his or her reaction is to get very emotional, the camera zooms to a close-up of the person's face. This is a reporter's dream. Try to avoid an emotional reaction like this. I would advise you to avoid any interview in which you might become emotional. It's too dangerous.

So, you are asked a question that just burns you up. You want to slug someone. Do not. Gather your self-confidence, smile and recite a nursery rhyme, out loud in front of the camera. Do or say something that cannot possibly be broadcast on television. Then, compose yourself. Often, the reporter's questions are not part of the broadcast. (Clue, the reporter is not in the camera's field of vision.) It is only your answer that is broadcast. You want to control the context within which you give an answer. Try this; ask yourself the question as your response, then respond at the same time. Your answer should contain both the question and answer. You then control the context. You are not avoiding the question but you are answering it in a way that will give you the best opportunity to answer appropriately. Just remember that both question and answer must be in sound bite format.

This same technique works for positive news stories also. It gives you the chance to enhance a question that may be a little flat and then respond with an enhanced answer.

Should the reporter be in the camera shot with you it may still be to your advantage to do something silly to divert the emotion you may feel at a given question. It won't be broadcast and you can take a minute to regroup and get control of the interview. The reporter needs something news worthy. Give them what you think is news worthy.

Reporters use various techniques to trip you up and try to "make" news. There are two examples that happened to me that are worth remembering.

The surprise.

I was once called by a television reporter and asked to meet them at a specific place at a specific time. At the organization I worked in, the entrance gate always notified the office when the press came in. I was notified the press had arrived quite awhile before my scheduled interview.

That is not all that unusual since television often shoots "B Roll" or background shots that can be used with the story.

This time I was curious and went to my scheduled place early. There, a reporter was interviewing a disgruntled employee who was very critical of something. I then had the advantage of hearing the interview to which I was asked to respond. The reporter wanted to confront me without my knowledge of what had been said previously. It was to have been a surprise! **The set up.**

In this example the reporter and camera operator set up two interviews that are not only different in the content but also very different in presentation. As with the surprise, the disgruntled employee is interviewed in the comfort of a warm living room. As the respondent, I was interviewed outside in 0 degree weather for over 30 minutes. The disgruntled employee's interview shots were of her sitting on a sofa. My interview shots were close up looks of my pale, nearly shivering face. It did not matter what was said. The look and feel of the camera angles and the location made the story the way the reporter wanted it to look. They had complete control. It was a manipulation of fact with interview and camera techniques, that are very difficult to change or control.

Be aware of the fact that reporters learn and use techniques to control the story. If you can't control the story yourself you must at least know what is happening and try to control the damage. Why didn't I insist on being interviewed in a warm cozy room? I wasn't aware of what was happening until it was over, and I saw the result.

Some organizations use professionals to deal with the press. It is a good idea if you have the advantage of someone who can do that. You must suppress the lure of being on camera or on radio or in the newspaper and trust the professional to do that work. A good manager uses professionals for the good of the organization. If they are not available, a good manager recognizes the advantages and disadvantages of the press and learns how to deal with them in an effective manner.

It might be possible to develop a relationship with a reporter that will provide you with an advantage when you need to get news out or when the press wants a story from you. Let's say that a newspaper reporter is assigned to cover your organization. Meet informally with the reporter, as often as you can. Coffee, lunch or just a few minutes to chat during the day are good ways to get to know the person. Be sure that you always contact that reporter when you have some news. If another reporter contacts you, put them off until you can talk to your reporter.

It is more difficult to develop a relationship with radio or television reporters. They often move around a lot. The type of organization you manage is often assigned to a summer intern so you don't really have a "regular" reporter. You might find a long-term employee in the news organization with whom you can get to know. If the news organization is helpful to your organization and you have a good relationship with the news staff, consider rewarding that news organization. For example, if your community has 4 television stations and one in particular is very good to your organization you might reward them with an exclusive story or they may be first on your list to call. You might give them a "heads up" on a story or some additional information. Be careful that you don't show too much favoritism. Balance your relationships with the news organizations. You don't want to make an enemy and, ideally, you want all the news organizations to be friendly and helpful to your organization. Spread the rewards around if it is warranted.

Chapter 3

A Manager Is

Before we get too far it is important to clarify what a manager is. A manager can be a division head, department head, CEO, Director, Executive Director among other titles. Throughout this book, manager is the term used to represent any and all of these titles. Many of the recommendations also apply to line managers and middle managers. Management is really a team effort and any person in an unmanageable organization can benefit from knowing about management survival in that organization.

A good manager, first and foremost, sets team and individual priorities based on the organization's vision and mission. This is accomplished through goals and objectives using performance standards, performance measures and other tools to ensure success. Here are definitions of the basics with more detail in later chapters:

- Vision—mental picture or imagination of the future of the organization.
- Mission—calling: The business of the organization.
- Goal—aim: a general, long-term objective associated with the mission.
- Objective or Key Result Area—a measurable step necessary to achieve a goal.

A manager can also be a leader. In fact, it is good to be both. Most people are not both and the qualities of each are different.

Leadership and Management

As a good manager you must possess certain skills and character that will assist in making management easier. There are two main qualities necessary for a good manager, leadership qualities and management qualities.

Leadership qualities

- Personal integrity–we all have limits to our behavior based on what we believe in and how we accept society's mores. A good leader has well defined and strong moral beliefs and behavior. A good leader follows the rules; both shaped internally and created by society. That does not mean that beliefs, behaviors and rules cannot be questioned, but when it comes down to doing, the good leader does what is right. A simple example is this: I decide that I will only cross an intersection when the pedestrian light says, "Walk". I never change that behavior. When I walk with a group of people or the Governor of the State, I do not cross unless the light says, "Walk". The group may leave me behind but I wait. Personal integrity can cause conflicts in management. Let's say your personal integrity, based on a religious belief, is against consuming alcohol. Your organization chooses to serve alcohol at a special event. Some managers in this situation would argue against serving alcohol and might resign if it is served. In fact, your personal integrity is not violated if your organization serves alcohol. It is violated if you consume alcohol at the event! Your personal integrity should not guide the organization but you will be a good leader if you have personal integrity and don't violate it.

- Honesty–tell the truth. It seems a simple matter but many people have a difficult time being honest. This is especially true when there are political pressures, a desire to shield your staff from bad news or a need to put off questioning press reporters. There are other reasons, as well, that you may be tempted to be less than honest. Don't succumb to these pressures. When found out, you will never escape the dishonesty. There are ways to deal with these pressures that are explored in other areas of this book. Good leaders are honest.

- Passion–for what your organization stands for–you must have passion for your organization's vision and mission. There are people who are just good managers. They can manage anything. "No, I've never worked in a museum but I've managed a copy center and a chain of pizza stores so I can manage the museum." Wrong! We are not talking about easily managed organizations. We are talking about unmanageable organizations. One of their characteristics is having a mission that is worthy, one that requires a passion for it. A "manager" cannot be truly effective because the passion isn't there. On the other hand, people with the passion don't necessarily make good managers. Having the passion and being a good manager is what this book is all about. It is the passion for the vision and mission and the ability to manage that make a good leader.

Management qualities:

- Ability to organize and direct–a good manager is an orchestra leader, directing, coordinating and merging the interests and talents of the organizational publics.
- Ability to talk to people—a good manager must be comfortable talking not only to the janitor in the organization but also the mover and shaker in the community.
- Empathy–learn to understand another's feelings as best you can. This ability allows you succeed with the above management qualities. This is a hard thing to do. We all have such varied experiences and influences in our lives. However, we all share the desire for a quality life, to be recognized for our efforts and be respected for our ideas.

- Know and be able to use technology–lots of managers don't feel any need to learn how to use technology and leave it up to others in the organization. No one can afford to do that these days. Understanding technology and how it can help the organization succeed is essential for a good manager.

There are other qualities of leadership and management that are outlined in lots of management articles and books. But these are a good start and I believe essential ones.

As a manager, you can never get enough training for the various skills necessary to carry out your job. A manager must have many, many skills and be able to provide the various publics involved in the organization with what they need: training in supervision, planning, working with people, budgeting, public speaking, technology, public relations, etc. Take advantage of as many training opportunities to learn as possible. Read the rest of this book too. It can't hurt.

Chapter 4

But I'm Not a Manager

A manager, first and foremost, facilitates the work of others. No matter what position you are in; you must be an active part of the organization. You must provide something for the manager to facilitate. In a team-oriented organization, you essentially run the organization. You must know how to do that and be proactive in your job.

The most difficult thing for any employee to face is change. Yet, if your organization is not constantly changing, it is failing. Change is what invigorates an organization, allows it to adjust to changing climates (politics) and provides necessary room for improvement.

During a change in your organization you may feel uncertain. You might start to mistrust other employees and your supervisors. You might feel you cannot depend on the organization. Communication may suffer along with productivity, even your own! Teams may start to be more protective of their own work areas. You may see power struggles emerging.

Is it time to bail out? No. This is time to think about what is going on, understand why there is change and show some real leadership in your organization. Leadership is not just restricted to managers. Your leadership will help managers facilitate the change and make the organization better.

There are some very important things you can do to understand change and assist your organization:

- How you react to any situation is your choice so control your attitude. Keep positive and don't allow others to bring you down. Help keep the good news flowing, not the bad.
- What you perceive to be mistakes by managers may not be so. Be tolerant of even real mistakes. A manager can never make everyone happy and some decisions are made for a manager by a governing authority. Understand this and become part of the solution by ensuring your co-workers know this.
- You should not work in an organization that does not change. So, expect it, welcome it. Be proactive and suggest changes yourself. Be flexible and understand that there are many ways to do something well.
- It is important to be extremely knowledgeable about the organization's vision, mission, key result areas, performance measures, etc. By knowing these things you can better understand why change is happening and know where changes will eventually lead.
- Your own professional growth can benefit from a change. Do not avoid an opportunity to grow because you don't like the change. Exhibiting good leadership during a change will be recognized.
- Change is not the end of the world. Keep a sense of humor and enjoy the ride. If you are fun to be around in your work place, your co-workers will accept changes better also.
- If changes do stress you, practice some stress management techniques. You might help your co-workers by showing them techniques that work for you.
- Change is no time to stop doing your job in the best possible way you can. Keep working for the organization and both you and the organization will benefit.

When I was an animal keeper at the Topeka Zoo, I was going to fill in for a keeper who was taking a two-week vacation. Because he was the primary keeper of the area, he showed me how to take care of the area and emphasized how important it was to do the job the same way he did it. I worked for several days on the job after he left for vacation and realized the routine was not very efficient. I made a change. I first checked with my supervisor and explained that I thought the work could get done in less time and be just as effective, if not more so. In addition, I would free up some time to work on special projects. I got the go ahead to "rearrange" the schedule and documented it. Sure enough, I could get the work done much faster and had free time for special projects.

The primary keeper returned and he was not happy. I showed him the procedure I used but he would not change. Several weeks later I learned that he had changed the routine, not as dramatically as I had, but still made a change. The change was for the good. The primary keeper resisted change for the reasons we all do but as he reflected on the benefits, he took it upon himself to adjust the work. He benefited and the organization benefited.

Later, I became a supervisor and told keepers that I felt that a routine could be done any way that suited them as long as the various time deadlines were met (e.g. animals fed when scheduled, animals on exhibit when scheduled).

A keeper approached me to complain that her routine had too much to do on it and I needed to relieve her of some of her responsibilities. I suggested that a change in the routine might free up some time. I had worked this routine some years before and thought it could be more efficient. She challenged me to work the routine and see for myself that it was too much for one person to do in a day.

There was a lot to do but I immediately noticed one thing that seemed ripe for change. A horse barn had to be cleaned out daily. The keeper would shovel the manure and hay into a wheelbarrow and push the wheelbarrow to an adjacent building then up a ramp into a trailer. The trailer was parked at the other building because of the large amount of material loaded into it from that building. I talked to the keepers in the other building to find a time that I could move the trailer. When it was convenient for them, I moved the trailer to the barn I was cleaning and loaded everything directly onto the trailer. This saved a lot of time and a lot of labor. When I told the complaining keeper about the way I cleaned out the barn, she said I was cheating and it wasn't a true test. It was just a change. If you are flexible enough to accept change, things can get better.

It is not just change that everyone has to deal with. There seems to be an innate mistrust of managers. You can curtail that mistrust by getting to know those people. Most are just like you with a family, a mortgage and bills to pay. Recognizing that, will go a long way towards understanding that everyone in an organization has a job to do, each with different responsibilities.

If you can learn to accept change, accept and trust managers and understand what the organization is all about; you can be a valuable asset to the organization and be a part of its success.

Maybe you work for a poor manager. They are out there often perpetuated and promoted by governing authorities that don't know any better. Here are a few tips to help you cope with a poor manager:

- Keep notes. Document what you do and what instructions you were given.
- If it hasn't happened, try to convince the organization to adopt teams as a way to manage day-to-day activities. This may be the very best way to deal with poor managers. Unfortunately, there may be a poor manager that will not relinquish control and prevent teams from working.
- Suggest that instructions or policy changes be given to the entire workgroup at once, not to you individually. Sometimes, individual instructions get tangled in personal feelings. Group meetings can control this.
- Keep focused on the organization's vision, mission, etc. If you can talk to the manager logically, ask how a given change in policy fits with the organization's vision, mission, etc. If you are knowledgeable

enough about these things, you might suggest a modification that better fits the mission.

- Suggest changes in such a way that it appears they are the manager's idea. You don't really need all the accolades, especially if the change is beneficial.
- Move on. It may be a tough decision but don't waste your career in an organization that is failing because a manager is poor.

I assume that, as an employee of an important organization, you want to excel. You want to be the best employee you can be and you want the organization to be successful and be on the cutting edge of innovation.

However, I must acknowledge that some of you may not want these things. I doubt you are reading this book but if you are you might find solace in just showing up for work each day, pushing some papers or shoveling something else and waiting for pay day. An organization with a government governing authority is your place to be. Mediocrity is accepted and you will get a pension that is pretty secure. It will be small but a steady income. If this is you, it will be a waste of time for you to continue this book.

For those of you that read on:

Be a good subordinate. You might be surprised how well you will succeed.

Do not be an antagonist.

Chapter 5

Antagonists

There will be a lot of people lined up to see you during your first days on the job. A few of them will be antagonists. It is best to be aware of this fact and to recognize them early on.

Antagonists are everywhere but seem to be more effective in unmanageable organizations. They may be more numerous also because unmanageable organizations are fertile ground for antagonists to work. They may be inside your organization or outside. Those outside usually recruit followers from inside the organization that act as information gatherers.

Antagonists are people who:

- Attack individuals who are usually in leadership positions.
- Make demands but are never satisfied.
- Manipulate or create information to discredit people or their performance.
- Have no remorse for the damage to people's careers or even to the organization they often pretend to support.
- Can be very likeable and easily put others at ease thus gaining their confidence.
- Are so convinced they are right that anyone who disagrees is wrong and can become a target.

Since a manager is the most likely target of an antagonist, it is important to know how to identify someone who is or could be an antagonist. It is easy to confuse an activist with an antagonist but here is a clue. An activist is *issue oriented*, attacking policies or procedures dealing with specific issues. An antagonist is *people oriented* attacking individuals, questioning their competence, their integrity or anything else that comes to mind. That doesn't mean that an antagonist might not use an issue as the basis to begin a personal attack but in the end the attack is always against individuals.

Here are a few clues that you have a problem with an antagonist:

- You've just been hired as the manager of an organization. Someone approaches you and tells you that the last manager was a real jerk and you will be able to finally get the organization back on track. Beware. You are most likely talking to an antagonist.

- A new employee greets you warmly and in your discussions you learn the employee has held jobs in many organizations and often left because they disagreed with "the administration." This is another likely antagonist.

- Someone claiming that a number of others are concerned about where the organization is headed approaches you. The "number of others" can't be named. This is an antagonist at work.

- You are at a public meeting when someone gets the floor and begins a long speech about "concerns" and "lack of leadership" and many other items. This is the antagonist's forum.

- A staff member is taking copious notes, especially when you are talking during a staff meeting. A possible antagonist or an antagonist's recruit is present.

Even though a manager is the most likely target of an antagonist, the antagonist is a problem for the entire organization; the staff, support groups, governing authority, etc. In too many organizations when an antagonist appears, everyone disassociates with the person being attacked and fails to recognize the danger. This plays into the hands of the antagonist and makes their job much easier. It allows the antagonist to continue because the person being attacked is isolated. The problem for the organization, then, becomes those who let the antagonist continue, not the person who is the antagonist.

As a manager of an unmanageable organization, you are particularly vulnerable to an attack from an antagonist. Many unmanageable organizations deal with emotionally charged issues such as artifact care, animal care, humane treatment, etc. Antagonists thrive in these types of organizations.

Government governing authorities are not only a prime place in which antagonists can work but government often encourages them. "Whistle blower" laws protect antagonists. That is not to say that honest, well-meaning whistle blowers should not be protected but antagonists should not. You must know the difference. There are many layers of people in the governing authority and a good antagonist can find one or more people that can be convinced that their view is correct. People in the governing authority can have a great deal of say about your future and if they are under the influence of an antagonist, your future is not bright.

I recall an incident in which a staff member who was an antagonist had violated personnel rules of the governing authority. Termination was recommended. The personnel department, as part of the termination process, interviewed her. Her skills as an antagonist resulted in the complete reversal of the termination and the beginning of a painful investigation of the organization and the resignation of a key supervisor who did no wrong. Antagonists are experts at influencing people and diverting blame to others. Managers run into this problem all the time and don't understand what happened. Suddenly, you are requested to provide documentation and explanations about things totally unrelated to the problem you were, at first, dealing with.

It is important for you, as a manager, to be able to recognize an antagonist. Unfortunately, that is often not enough. If others in your organization, in your support group or your governing authority can't recognize an antagonist, you are vulnerable. A good antagonist knows this and will find people who can easily be convinced that you are the scum of the earth.

Antagonists use a variety of means to convince others that you are a problem. Some of those means include:

- Letters to the editor of newspapers
- Television and radio
- Letter writing campaigns to people and other organizations
- E-mail campaigns
- Web sites
- Petitions to government agencies
- Meetings with key community leaders to discuss "problems"
- Making comments at public meetings of the organization, its support group and/or its governing authority

There are other means as well but as you might imagine, an antagonist who uses one or more of these means can create extreme difficulties for you. You can easily be consumed by trying to deal with inquiries, with explanations, with your own defenses that your job becomes impossible. If you can't get anything done in your job, you just add to the fodder the antagonist needs to build a case against you.

Another advantage the antagonist has is that people tend to believe him/her rather than you. There are several reasons for this:

- Bad news creates headlines. Good news does not
- The truth is seldom as interesting as half truths or made up stories
- Many people would rather believe something bad about you rather than something good
- The antagonist may be mistaken for an activist
- Many line employees automatically assume that management and managers are wrong

The only real defense against these things is education. Everyone who is associated with an organization must be educated about antagonists, how to recognize them, how to deal with them and how not to deal with them. This is more than a daunting task. It may well be impossible in your organization. However, it may be one of the most important tasks you face as a manager.

Dealing with an antagonist is difficult in an unmanageable organization because the way you deal with them is often out of your hands. Conflict resolution will not work yet you might be required to engage in that exercise. Answering accusations point-by-point is also a waste of time and may give the antagonist more information to use against you. Yet, you may be required to do this by a supervisor, governing authority, government oversight agency, etc. These requirements put you at a disadvantage and only encourage the antagonist. You find yourself not working to defuse the antagonist but trying to convince others not to play into the plans of the antagonist.

In some unmanageable organizations, government oversight agencies are required to investigate any and all complaints, even frivolous ones. The very fact that this agency begins an investigation gives the antagonist some validity and those investigations quickly become part of the information provided to the media, staff, support organizations, governing authority and others. It does not matter whether the investigation does not find anything wrong, it just matters that one was conducted. The antagonist can be so overwhelming to those who fail to recognize they are being used that they will commit wrongful acts to get the antagonist off their back. An investigator once told me that they were required to find something wrong during an investigation because their "superiors" wanted to appease the antagonist.

How can you survive an antagonist? It is difficult and sometimes not worth it. However here are a few tips:

- Prevent attacks by educating those associated with your organization
- Be able to recognize antagonists and work to prevent their influence
- Maintain your professional behavior

- Try to keep your concentration on the organization's vision and mission
- Document all you do and say
- Find a key community leader to advise you
- Become so politically powerful in the community that an antagonist can't harm you

The last point is actually the only way you can be confident of your survival should an antagonist attack. Unfortunately, this often requires you to be a long time manager in the organization with community connections that give you the necessary political power. Government governing authorities have recognized this and don't like people who have this kind of political power. They feel threatened and will sometimes recruit or support an antagonist to eliminate this threat. If an antagonist can find even tacit support from a Governor, a Mayor, a County Commissioner, a City Council Member or any other high ranking political or staff member, they have tools nearly impossible to counter.

If your organization is lucky enough to not have antagonists, it is a blessing to not have to deal with them. Just remember that they can crop up at any time and you must be prepared. The fact that you work in an unmanageable organization increases the likelihood that you will have to deal with an antagonist. Hope for a poor antagonist because a good one will end your career and severely damage the organization and smile about what they accomplished. The organization has to realize that just because you are gone does not mean the end of the antagonist. The target just changes and the cycle repeats itself.

Chapter 6

Staffing

Staffing can make or break an organization and a manager's career. Unfortunately, unmanageable organizations often have hiring and firing policies that make it nearly impossible to hire the right staff or fire unproductive or inappropriate staff. These policies are usually those of the parent organization. Government is the worst offender in this area. It is true, in many governments, that once you are hired, you have the job for life. Managers are excluded from this truism, however. (Be careful). Performance matters little and appropriateness to the organization's core activities is not considered.

I have personally watched an employee who received ones and twos, the low end of a ten-point performance rating scale, not only remain in the job but also be promoted to the highest level of the organization. Unmanageable organizations are made so in part because governing authorities and politicians reward mediocrity and rid themselves of excellence.

If the organization's focus core activity (Chapter 13 defines core and focus activities) is very specialized, such as a Zoo, it may seem necessary to hire a staff that specializes in caring for that focus. In the case of a Zoo, one would hire animal and plant specialists such as zookeepers and horticulturists. However, one of the elements that make an organization unmanageable is that the majority of the staff is concerned with the organization's focus core activity and not the primary core activity, customer care.

I believe managers should reconsider staffing their organizations with people who specialize in the focus activity of the organization. Rather, staffing should emphasize abilities in customer care then knowledge of the focus activity. This could be likened to having a major in customer care and a minor in the focus activity.

Ideally a manager should be able to start with a fresh, hand picked staff that fully supports the vision, mission and core activities of the organization. That just doesn't happen. One of your tasks, as a good manager, is to attempt to mold your staff into a team that supports the organization's vision, mission and core activities.

There are a lot of management books written about teamwork and all the various methods to create a team and ensure they work together. But as a manager, you need to realize a very important aspect of human behavior. There is nothing that unifies a group of people more than a common enemy. A common enemy unites people to support a government or movement. Broad support for a war would not be possible without a common enemy. In business, the common enemy may be a competitor.

The lack of a common enemy in many organizations adds to the difficulty in managing them and is an obstacle to creating a well functioning team. Unfortunately, an organization's administration often becomes the common enemy for the staff. As the manager and the representative of the administration, the common enemy is you. This is why unions work. They create a common enemy, management, and unite the workforce against the common enemy.

As a good manager you must find a way to overcome your organization's lack of a common enemy and create a team that will work together for the shared vision and mission of the organization. Here are some steps to creating teamwork in your organization:

- Have a shared vision and mission that everyone supports. This is accomplished through the process of creating a vision and mission.

- Create teams within the organization with specific responsibilities.
- Train staff on the functions and operations of a team. For example, here is a code of conduct for team meetings:
  1. Attend all team meetings
  2. Leave all titles at the door
  3. Learn and use the problem solving techniques
  4. Work on job-related problems in the area of responsibility and expertise of the team
  5. Personalities will not be discussed
  6. Listen to the ideas of others and keep an open mind
  7. Attempt to reach a consensus on all decisions
  8. Stick to the Agenda for the meeting
  9. Participate fully during the meeting
  10. Volunteer for and complete Action Items and other assignments
  11. Every Member shares responsibility for the progress of the team
  12. Be on time and do not leave early
- Empower teams to make organizational decisions. This is tough for a manager to do. There are some decisions you must reserve to make on your own. Your parent organization or governing authority requires that you be responsible. The most difficult part of empowering a team to make decisions is taking responsibility for the decisions. It requires the team to function completely in sync with the organization's vision, mission and core activities such that, as a manager, you can take responsibility for the team's decisions in complete confidence.
- Recognize each team's contributions to the organization's success. This recognition must be meaningful to the staff members. Pubic recognition is the most rewarding. Along with that may be bonuses, workplace perks or promotions.
- Don't ignore team responsibilities in an organization's failure. Retrain, refocus and encourage the team to ensure future successes.

In an organization with highly functioning teams, the managers become facilitators for the teams, providing resources for the teams that will allow teams to make the best organizational decisions. Highly functioning teams make managing an unmanageable organization much easier because teams take on the bulk of the decision-making. Staff members are empowered by the team and feel they are a vital part of the organization. They are recognized for their contributions to the organization's successes. They work as a team for the good of the organization.

Teams are formed in two major categories; functional and cross-functional.

Functional teams are formed with staff in a specific functional area of the organization. A Facility Management Team would be made up of facility care staff and be responsibility for the core activity of facility care. A narrower functional team may concern itself with a program area such as a Conservation Management Team within the core activity of collection care.

Cross-functional teams are formed with staff from a variety of functional areas of the organization. In recent years, Quality Management Teams have been popular in many organizations. These teams have members from a number of functional areas and are usually formed to study a particular process. They are often disbanded when the study is completed. For example, the process of purchasing may be studied for improvement by a cross-functional team made up of members from the Facility Care Team, the Customer Care Team and the Collection Care Team. In large organizations with a parent organization and a number of sub organizations, representatives from all the organizations may make up the team. This is especially true for processes that affect all the organizations.

Using teams to improve processes and make organizational decisions can be very effective in managing the unmanageable organization. The downside is that the team method is not very efficient. Some decisions must be made quickly without the necessary time to organize a team or for the team to meet to discuss the decision. One way to deal with this problem is to create a cross-functional team to study the decision making process and set up procedures by which certain decisions can be made by a manager outside the team decision making process. Once again this empowers staff to be a part of all decision-making. It is a powerful, unifying force.

Before teams are formed, it is necessary for issues or processes for improvement to be identified and clearly stated. These "output statements" might be developed by a manager or a management team. The Key Result Areas of the organization (see Chapter 12) may generate them. In a highly team oriented organization output statements might be generated by a specialized team formed for this specific purpose. Teams are generally formed to solve problems or improve quality or both.

Quality Management as a team function bears some additional examination. There are many books written about this topic. Essentially, the idea is that all processes in an organization can be improved. The improvement of each process is never totally complete and is an ongoing method of management. This is often referred to as Continuous Quality Improvement. For example, an organization forms a quality management team to improve the process of purchasing. The team determines that a better way to purchase is to use a bank managed credit card rather than purchase orders and checks. After the transition to credit cards the team reexamines the process to ensure credit card purchases are better managed by creating oversight procedures. Continuous improvement may also be necessary due to changes in laws or governing authority rules that affect procedures. Quality teams may be permanent or reformed when necessary.

Teams go through several stages of development before they can truly become highly functional.

- Forming–In this stage the team forms with members determined by what type of team is involved. Functional teams will have members from the functional unit of the organization while cross-functional teams will have members from a variety of functional units. Members are also determined by the span of the team's concern. If the team's charge is to look at a particular problem or process of a unit of the organization, team members will be from that unit of the organization. On the other hand, if the problem or process involves several units or several organizations, team members will come from several units or organizations. This is also the stage where a team leader, team recorder and other necessary positions are selected.

- Storming–This stage occurs after the team is initially formed. It is a normal process of team members defining their own place on the team. This can be a very volatile but necessary process. The team leader must be careful to control this process but not suppress it. It is a time when team members get to know one another and learn how each will contribute to the team.

- Normalizing–After the dust has settled from the storming stage the team evolves into normal activity. Team members have learned how to interact with and recognize the strengths and weaknesses of each other. Team meetings are relaxed and can begin to focus on the issues the team was formed to consider.

- Performing–In order to perform well, a team must go through the previous stages of development. In the last stage, performing, the team works well together and is able to produce meaningful results. The strengths of each team member contribute to the process and the team not only learns but also effectively uses problem solving and improvement techniques. A highly functional, performing team is an asset to the organization and helps make it successful. It also makes your job as manager much easier.

Unfortunately, when individual team members change the stages of team development start over. They may not take as long as the initial team took but must still occur. Well functioning teams may wonder why they suddenly are unable to perform when a new team member arrives or an old team member is replaced. Every team must recognize the process of becoming a performing team and must go through all the stages of development for every new team member.

Being a good supervisor. Being a good subordinate.

If you are a manager you are most likely also a supervisor. Self directed work teams may help mitigate your supervisory duties but probably will not eliminate them. Governing authorities usually require employee evaluations, attendance reports, payroll hours and many other things required of you as a supervisor. There are many books and many training courses available to teach supervisory skills. Avail yourself of these and learn all you can.

You might be surprised, however, that being a good subordinate is harder than being a good supervisor. For one thing, you will not find many books or training courses on the subject. While we've all been a "subordinate," the level at which you are changes the characteristics of your subordination. Being the "low person on the totem pole" is a lot different than being the "top banana." As you "climb the ladder" there will be less supervision of you and more latitude and freedom to make decisions without oversight.

I left an organization where I was "top banana" and began working at an organization where I was "low person on the totem pole." It was difficult and I had to do a lot of soul searching to find a way to be comfortable with my new role. I decided to think about how I would want my subordinate to act if I were in my supervisor's position. So, when asked by my supervisor about my thoughts on what project to work on, (she was good enough to ask, a good supervisor) my response was, "Let's work on a project that benefits the organization and helps meet your supervisor's expectations of your job performance." A good subordinate works for the good of the organization and works to ensure the success of their supervisor. The payoff can be immense, maybe not always in pubic recognition, but always in personal satisfaction.

Chapter 7

Volunteers

Many unmanageable organizations supplement their operations by using volunteers. Volunteers are often used to provide services that are not funded in the organization's operating budget or to add value to programs that don't have adequate funding. Volunteers are also used to involve the community in the organization and often draw volunteers from the organization's support group.

Unmanageable organizations are usually under funded. They often want to provide services and programs within their vision and mission but fail to receive adequate financial support for them. Volunteers help fill this need.

Some organizations have a staff member that recruits and coordinates volunteers. In others, a support group may provide volunteer services for the organization. In still others, the volunteers themselves organize and become a support group whose only function is providing volunteers, often for a special program or service.

In all cases, it is important for the organization to clearly define volunteer needs of the organization, qualifications necessary for volunteers and how those volunteers will operate within the organization. Some organizations will accept any warm body if they agree to volunteer. This is not a good practice. Other organizations develop job descriptions for each volunteer position that defines the expectations of the organization for the volunteer. This is by far the best way to obtain good volunteers. The hardest thing to do with a volunteer is "fire" them. However, it is sometimes necessary to do so. That is much easier if there is a written set of expectations and an evaluation of each volunteer in which meeting those expectations is measured. Volunteers are much like employees in this sense.

Volunteer recognition is both important and, at times, complicated. Everyone wants to be recognized but the organization must ensure the recognition is appropriate and within the resources of the budget. A good manager never misses an opportunity to publicly recognize volunteers. While often informal, this type of recognition is vitally important. Organizations may have an annual recognition banquet that recognizes the contributions of volunteers by hours of donated time or years of donated service. There may be prizes or certificates but the most important part is the public recognition. Inviting volunteers to previews or openings of new exhibits for program kick offs is another way to ensure they feel they are important to the organization.

People of many different ages and backgrounds are attracted to volunteerism. Your organization will undoubtedly be tested by some of these people. Volunteer organizations are good places for antagonists to work. Be aware of this. It is also important to recognize that expectations for volunteers must be tempered with knowledge of work ethics of various age groups, available times and the value of the volunteer contributions. It is not unusual to find that the return on the investment in the volunteer or volunteer group is not worth it. My first advice is to do what you can to make the investment worth it and secondly consider abolishing the volunteer program. Don't do the latter unless you can really justify it and have thick skin. You may need to factor in the difficulties of abolishing the volunteer program when considering the return on investment. That could tip the scale in favor of keeping it. Certainly, the most effort should be put in making the volunteer program successful. There is much to be gained from a volunteer program that is strong and provides the organization with expertise and assistance when needed.

Chapter 8

Governance

Unmanageable organizations have a governing authority. They are established to provide organizational oversight, public input and ensure the organization conforms to rules and regulations. Inherent in a governing authority is politics and political processes. There is nothing that makes an organization as unmanageable as does the governing authority.

There are different types of governing authorities. They range from government to organizational boards. They differ mostly in their focus but also in their stability.

Government is the most unfocused and unstable type of governing authority. On a local level, government's functions are basically to gather and spend constituent resources, provide for constituent wants and set rules and regulations for constituent behaviors. Constituents are the general public within the government's domain but may also include special interest groups. Functions change somewhat as one moves to State and Federal governments but only in that some additional functions are added. The basic ones are part of all levels of government.

Government has no focus. It cannot because government is driven by constituent wants. Wants change constantly. Constituents want the focus to be on crime reduction one day then the next day want the focus to be on better streets. Wants are often recognized only if they get the attention of the politicians elected to represent the constituents. Unfortunately, many politicians have their own agendas that may or may not be representative of the majority of the constituents thus creating a further failure to focus.

Politicians are elected. They are defeated. Government changes. One election may change the entire flavor of the government. It is, in this sense, unstable as a governing authority.

Your organization needs to focus, to have a stable governing authority in order to accomplish your vision and mission. It is a miracle that so many organizations survive pretty well with government as a governing authority. But it is tough. Your organization and you, as its manager, are as near failure as you ever will be. You just may not be aware of it. If you are in an organization with government as your governing authority, tread carefully, and be prepared. The chances you will be leaving before you want to are high. The chances your organization will realize its vision and mission are slim.

The most focused and stable governing authority is one that is formed for the sole purpose of providing the resources and policies for the organization. A Library Board that has the authority to levy taxes, issue bonds, hire staff and set the organizational policies of the Library is an example. This type of governing authority must have statutory authorization to collect and expend resources, among other things. Members of the Board may be appointed by political bodies such as government subdivisions or even selected by peer board members. Generally, these board members are appointed or selected because of their interest and commitment to the organization. They accept and work for the organization's vision and mission. The Board is usually stable due to overlapping terms and is focused due to the type of individual who participates. If you have an opportunity to work for this type of governing authority, do not hesitate.

The Library Board example is the most extreme on the positive side of governing authorities. There are an infinite number of variations of this type of governing authority, however. One that I have seen become popular with Zoos is the development of a contract between the government governing authority and the Zoo support group (Zoo Society) for receiving tax subsidies and managing the organization. This has worked well in a number of communities but is certainly dependent on how well the contract is written and the amount of political influence the government retains.

Government does not easily relinquish power especially when money is involved. It is not uncommon for government to ask for several positions on the society's board. In the worst case, these positions become political appointments for individuals with no real interest in the organization. Board members with no real commitment hinder the necessary focus and stability of the organization.

It may seem a natural fit to contract with an organization's support group (Zoo Society) to manage the organization but, in fact, that may not be the best answer. Support groups are often formed with their own agendas, with a differing vision and mission from the organization itself. The support group may not wish to accept the organization's vision and mission but instead continue with its own. There are many examples of this clash in Zoos around the country.

Let's consider an example that is actually quite common in the Zoo world. A small Zoo's governing authority is city government. Red flags should be going up now. This is an organization that is highly unmanageable because the governing authority is unfocused and unstable. The organization has a support group, commonly called a Zoo Society or "Friends of" group. It is a membership group with a board of directors that selects their own members. In other words, no one is appointed to this board by the governing authority or any other group.

One purchases a membership to get some benefit, some return on the membership fee. In this case the benefits are:

- Free admission to the Zoo
- A newsletter

- One or more special events that are member only
- Satisfaction in assisting the Zoo

The support group has the advantage of being able to handle non-governmental resources; private donations; fund raising projects and various expenditures that are not regulated by the governing authority. This can be a real benefit to the organization.

There are costs to the organization for the support group to exist. A few are:

- Lost admission revenue
- Office space and utilities
- Staff time to assist the support group

The organization generally has no control over the revenues and expenditures of the support group. The support group's first priority for expenditures is to maintain its own operation. Supporting the needs of the organization it is supporting is a lower priority and in some cases can be a very low priority. The organization must request support from the support group's board of directors that can accept or reject the organization's request. In this example, there is nothing that requires the board of directors to be sympathetic of the organization's vision, mission or need for support. The support group is independent and as long as they can sell memberships and acquire donations, the support group can continue to exist, in extreme cases, without providing any support to the organization. Extreme cases do exist.

This example is a very difficult situation to be involved in if you are the manager of the organization. It is possible to get the attention of the support group by doing a cost/benefit analysis of the relationship between the organization and the support group. This cost/benefit analysis has to be done from the organization's standpoint. The support group either should not exist or should make significant changes if the cost/benefit to the organization is negative.

This is a simple cost/benefit analysis:

<u>Costs to the Organization</u>

Value of office space/yr	$ 25,500
Value of utilities	$ 1,500
Value of member visits	$137,500
includes lost rev & cost to service visitor	
Value of staff support	$ 3,000
Total cost to organization	**$167,500**

<u>Benefits to Organization</u>

Education Program	$ 57,184
Conservation Program	$ 7,600
Marketing	$ 13,000
Direct Operating Support	$ 5,000
Special Events	$ 35,500
Membership Service	$ 37,000
Publications	$ 9,000
Total Benefit	**$164,284**
Difference	**$(3,216)**

In this example, there is a negative benefit to the organization. When one factors in revenues generated by the organization that directly support some of the programs that benefit the organization but are provided by the support group, a more negative cost/benefit results. There is no guarantee that this analysis will change anything but it is a valuable tool that might be a catalyst for some necessary changes. A good manager tracks costs and benefits using measurement tools discussed elsewhere.

How does a manager deal with the various governing authorities? If you are lucky enough to be working in an organization with a governing authority like the Library example, it is easier but you can't be complacent. It is imperative to be vigilant and proactive with the governing authority. Members of that governing authority must always be individuals that honestly support the organization's vision and mission and share in the passion for the organization's focus. This is accomplished through thorough screening and selection processes. One individual in this governing authority who promotes his or her own agenda, or is an antagonist, can seriously damage the organization. It has happened to good organizations many times.

If you are the manager of an organization with government as the governing authority, there are things you can do to help your organization but they can be dangerous. Basically, you have to become politically involved. That doesn't necessarily mean partisan politics. It does mean you must carefully scrutinize candidates for your governing authority and determine their views on your organization's vision and mission and the extent they are willing to support it. If the candidate is good for your organization, support him or her. There may be legal restraints on the type of support you can give but there are many ways to do so. The danger here is that your support could backfire. The candidate you support is not elected and in that person's place is someone not supportive of your organization. That's what makes your organization so unmanageable. You cannot predict the governing authority.

Additionally, it is a good idea to become involved in the community. Join a service organization and be active in it. Volunteer your time for community events either through your service organization or at large. Become a member of the local Chamber of Commerce and participate in their events. You might consider becoming active in an organization that is related to yours but not directly. For example, if your organization depends on public visitation you might become active in the local visitors bureau or tourism office. If your management position is in marketing you might join the local marketing group. The point is that it is important for you, as a manager, to be involved in you community whether that involvement is related to your organization or not. You will become better known in the community, but more importantly, you will develop friendships and relationship with others in the community that could become an asset to your organization outside the governing authority.

There is another way to thwart bad intentions by a government governing authority but this is rare indeed. The manager must be so popular and well known in the community that the governing authority cannot create problems for the organization in fear of their own political future. This is rare enough that I do not think you, as a manager, should count on this method to overcome the difficulties of the government governing authority.

Chapter 9

Strategic Planning

Not again! I used to hate the mere mention of strategic planning until I discovered how simple it is. Most managers struggle through the process of strategic planning, produce a report, put it on a shelf and forget it. That is not planning for the future; that is planning to fail. The real purpose of strategic planning is to train you to think strategically and work strategically.

Strategic planning consists of three main elements. First, figure out where you want to be at some time in the future (visioning). Second, determine where you are today (evaluation). Third, define the steps necessary to get from where you are today to where you want to be (goals and objectives). These three steps can be successfully applied to your personal life, your whole organization and even small units or projects within an organization.

A strategic plan for your personal life can be fairly simple. For example, let's say that I envision myself as being wealthy. That is my vision. I want to become wealthy through honesty and hard work. That is my mission. I believe that one of the things that will make me wealthy is to have at least $500 in a savings account in 5 years. That's a goal. Today, I don't have a savings account. That's where I am today. To accomplish one of my goals I must set up steps to get from where I am today to where I want to be in 5 years. These are my objectives. For example:

- Vision: To be wealthy.
- Mission: I will only become wealthy through honesty and hard work.
- Goal: Have at least $500 in a savings account in 5 years.
    o Objectives:
        - Open a savings account within 30 days.
        - Savings account will have a balance of at least $100 at the end of year 1.
        - Savings account will have a balance of at least $200 at the end of year 2.
        - Savings account will have a balance of at least $300 at the end of year 3.
        - Savings account will have a balance of at least $400 at the end of year 4.
        - Savings account will have a balance of at least $500 at the end of year 5.

Each objective is measurable, can be easily tracked and, if met, will accomplish the goal.

Did I accomplish my vision? If my definition of "wealthy" is limited to having $500 in a savings account then I accomplished it. If I saved $500 honestly and with hard word I accomplished my vision within the framework of my mission.

This simple example uses a number of terms in need of definition.

- Vision–mental picture or imagination of the future of the organization.
- Mission–calling: an aim or task that somebody believes is a duty to carry out or to which special importance is attached and requires special care. The business of the organization.
- Goal–aim: a general, long-term objective associated with the mission.
- Key Result Area or Objective–a measurable step necessary to achieve a goal. Also known as a Key Result Area.

An organization can have a mission without a strategic plan. Unfortunately, this scenario seems to be popular with many organizations. The organization is doing something within a framework but doesn't know where it is headed nor can it measure its progress. Likewise, a mission is not a requirement of a strategic plan. Good management dictates though, that a strategic plan be in place within the framework of a mission.

Applying this simple idea of strategic planning to an organization may seem daunting. In contrast to a personal strategic plan, an organization's plan must be created by consensus of many, if not all, the various interest groups or "publics" that an organization serves. A Zoo, for example, might have these publics to include in the planning process:

- Governing authority
- Financial supporters (taxpayer, donors, corporate sponsors, etc.)
- Government regulators
- Professional organizations (establish accrediting or standards of operation)
- Support organizations (membership partners)
- Community
- Staff
- Visitors

These are just a few of the publics but are ones most likely to be included in the planning process. Getting all these publics together and then to reach a consensus on a vision, a mission, etc. is a challenge but well worth the effort.

There is an inherent weakness in strategic planning for an unmanageable organization that you must keep in mind. Publics change, especially governing authorities and especially government governing authorities. What was consensus one day may not be the next. This weakness does not automatically doom strategic planning but you must establish a process of periodic review and revision, if necessary, to accommodate changing publics. This is not only good management but also necessary management to increase your chances of surviving an unmanageable organization and ensuring your organization's future success.

Chapter 10

Creating a Mission Statement

As a manager you must first clearly understand the difference between a vision and a mission. A vision is what you imagine your organization will be in the future. A mission is a statement that provides the framework under which that vision will be achieved. For example, Johnny Appleseed's vision may have been:

"To see the entire country covered with apple trees."

His mission would be:

"To plant as many apple seeds as possible in an environmentally and legally acceptable manner."

The mission is what you do to accomplish what you foresee as the end product.

The best place to start the process of creating a mission statement is to gather some background information about the organization. Most organizations have a parent organization or a professional organization of which they are a member. Your organization's mission and vision cannot run counter to the parent or professional organization but must complement them. Find out what those statements are and borrow from them. Not only will that help your organization get started but it also shows you are team players supporting the larger organization.

For example, if your organization is a subsidiary of Johnny Appleseed but your business is making apple cider you might share the same vision but your mission would be different. However, you might incorporate the environmental and legal parts of the mission to complement the parent organization.

If there is no parent or professional organization check the bylaws and charter of your organization. There you will find clues that will help in creating the mission statement.

A mission statement is most valuable when participation in creating it is maximized. This can be accomplished several ways. Two of the most common tools used to garner participation are surveys and focus groups.

Surveys involve developing a set of questions that will give the participant the opportunity to provide information relevant to creating a mission statement. This can be a very difficult task and is often contracted to a professional who knows the proper way to frame a question to get the desired information. I recommend having a professional create the survey questions.

Some organizations mail the survey to either representatives of their publics or at random. Other organizations target specific individuals that represent key publics (e.g. major donors) for a "one on one" interview and ask the survey questions. Still other organizations use both survey methods. Doing both types of survey has the advantage of gathering input from a broad range of participants as well as specific participants that may be the key to the success of your organization. If you must choose between one type of survey or another, choose the interview survey with representatives of the key publics.

Focus groups are groups of people gathered together to focus on a specific problem or question. They can effectively be used to create a mission statement and incorporate discussion, give and take and problem solving. Limited focus groups usually consist of a small number of participants and are often used to look at one or a few specific issues. They could be used to discuss one element of a mission. I don't recommend using a limited focus group to create a mission statement because you need as much participation as possible to create the mission statement. Limited focus groups are better used for creating goals and objectives.

A major focus group incorporates the most representatives and the most direct participation of the organization's publics. It is usually a large gathering with a facilitator. The facilitator guides the group through the process of creating the mission statement with broad-based consensus and support.

Larger organizations may hire an outside facilitator. The advantage to an outside consultant is that they don't have a vested interest in the outcome and can be more objective in the process. In a smaller organization, you, as a manager, may be the default facilitator. A good manager should work for the organization's best interests, not his or her own, and convey that effectively to the organization's publics. A good manager should be able to be the facilitator and, using the tools presented here, facilitate the creation of a mission statement. If an outside facilitator is hired, a good manager will be able to convey the organization's purpose, its professional standing and publics to the facilitator.

As the manager you have gathered some good background information and set up a major focus group with representatives of the publics that most affect your organization.

As the facilitator you are ready to guide the focus group to create a mission statement.

Here are some recommended steps to get the meeting started and functioning:

- Welcome the participants and introduce yourself.
- Have participants introduce themselves.
- Break the ice by playing a game. There are lots of games that can be played. Here are just two as examples:
  - For a small group, have participants pair off and interview each other. After the interviews each person introduces the person they interviewed to the whole group.

- o   For a large group, have all the participants stand. Throw a nerf ball to one person and have them give their name and name two interests they have unrelated to the organization. When that person is done they can throw the ball to another person and sit down. The holder of the ball repeats the introduction, throws the ball to another and sits down. This is repeated until all individuals are introduced.
- Clearly state (write out on an easel pad or similar) what is to be accomplished.
- Provide the background information previously collected.
- Establish some guidelines and limits for the creation process. For example, the mission must be stated in a short and concise statement. You might even set a number of words that cannot be exceeded.
- Begin the process.

One of the most popular tools that can be used in the process of creating a mission statement is brainstorming. To use brainstorming, it is important that all participants understand how to use it. Try using a practice brainstorming session to get everyone in the right mindset. Use two paper cone cups. This is the focus of the session. Then ask each participant to give an idea for using the cups. (To plant flowers. To drink from. Etc.) Write down each idea. Continue to get ideas until no one can think of any more. If the group is large you might limit the ideas to two ideas per participant.

The next step is to narrow the ideas to a manageable number. In this exercise the group must agree on the five most practical uses for the paper cups. Each participant then selects their top five ideas and rates them by putting a 5 next to their top choice, a 4 next to their second choice and so on. When all participants have voted, the points are tallied and the five with the most votes are listed on a fresh page on the easel pad.

You may only need two ideas. Just use the same voting technique to further narrow the list of five ideas to two.

After the exercise it is time to create the mission statement. Here is a good question for the group to focus on and provide ideas:

What is the purpose of our organization?

Each participant gets one or more chances to provide ideas for this question. Narrow the list using the voting tool used in the exercise. (e.g. each participant ranks their top five choices by placing a 5 beside their top choice, a 4 beside their next choice, etc. At the end the number all tallied and the 5 largest vote getters are selected.) The group should decide how many ideas to incorporate in the mission but this decision must be under the guidance of the facilitator. A facilitator must ensure that previously established guidelines and limits are enforced. When there are a number of publics represented there is a tendency for each public to want their idea adopted. Succumbing to that influence produces a poor mission statement.

Once a small number of ideas are adopted, they must be written into a simple, coherent statement. I recommend having an accomplished writer write the statement. Group writing can be a disaster and take up a lot of time for little gain. The focus group should know at the outset that they are not responsible for writing the statement; rather, they are responsible for creating the ideas that become the mission statement.

Here is an example of a poor mission statement. It is actually a vision statement and mission statement into one with few limits:

The Vision of the "organization" is to improve quality of life by providing safe, enjoyable, and attractive facilities, with diverse programs and efficient and responsive services, which enhance neighborhoods and encourage citizens to view the organization as a valued investment in their daily lives. To implement the vision, the organization will:

- Provide the highest level of measured customer satisfaction by meeting their needs, while encouraging open communication and exchange, dedicated to continuous improvement in delivering accessible services.

- Develop an ongoing marketing strategy that promotes and educates the public on all aspects of the organization including a specific marketing plan for each facility and program area.
- Actively seek and implement market-driven programs and events targeted for youth, families, and seniors, while maintaining our continued commitment to the entire community.
- As stewards, commit to respect, manage, evaluate, upgrade, and conserve the organization's human, cultural and natural resources, equipment, and facilities.
- Efficiently administer performance standards to meet capacity requirements for programs, facilities, and services by reducing barriers and maximizing the use of resources to create a greater economic impact within the Community.
- Maximize the use of volunteers and seek innovative alliances and partnerships with service providers that develop advocacy and sharing of resources by eliminating duplication to improve efficiency and productivity.
- Create appropriate benefit-based fee structures, through innovative revenue strategies that actively seek sponsorships and other earned revenue opportunities.
- Efficiently manage funding for improvements to enhance existing facilities and research the need for new lands, amenities, private involvement, and identify additional funding resources to meet the needs of the community.
- Create an environment of mutual trust and teamwork that coordinates resources to provide more cross training opportunities and job enrichment that improves flexibility and efficiency in a diverse workplace.
- Commit to implement meaningful professional and personal growth opportunities that enhance job satisfaction and generate improved service delivery.

In contrast, here are some examples of good mission statements because they are concise and clearly state the aim or task of the organization:

- United Community Center is a 501(c)(3) human service agency providing emergency assistance, daycare, social services and recreational activities for low-income children and families at risk in the inner city.

- Spacelabs Medical's mission is to be the leading worldwide provider of quality, cost-effective systems that gather, analyze, and present clinical information beneficial to the delivery of healthcare.

- The mission of the Compensation Advisory Organization of Michigan is to enhance the Michigan Workers' Compensation System through customer service, education and the administration of the Michigan Workers' Compensation Placement Facility.

- The Center for Academic Enrichment coordinates academic support and offers course work which helps students acquire the basic reading/writing and mathematics skills they will need to succeed in college.

- To provide needed quality leisure activities and facilities for the community that are effective and efficient.

- The mission of the Department of Public Health is to provide quality learning experiences and professional preparation for students, and to promote excellence in learning, teaching, scholarship and community service.

Remember a mission statement is an aim or task that somebody believes is a duty to carry out or to which special importance is attached and requires special care. It is the business of the organization.

Chapter 11

Creating a Vision Statement

A vision is a mental picture or imagination of the future of the organization. The process can be the same as the process of creating a mission statement and can be done with the same major focus group after the mission statement is created. It is important that the difference between a mission and vision are well understood by the group. The vision is where the organization will be in the future. The focus question may be:

Where do you see this organization is 10 years?

How do you envision this organization in 10 years?

Envision the future. Imagine what the organization should look like in the future. This is a time to be lofty and grand. Here are some good vision statements:

- Building a Safer Community Through Education.
- Serving beyond expectations.
- To be a Church that changes the world..........one life at a time.
- To exceed our customer's expectations and be the low cost producer.
- Our entrepreneurial culture creates value for our shareholders.
- Powering the Information Age.
- To be all that you can be.

Using a major focus group to create a mission and a vision statement results in a "Shared Mission" and a "Shared Vision." This is extremely important in managing the unmanageable organization. It is the glue that holds it all together. When publics are consistent and their members share the mission and vision, the organization will succeed. There is a sense of ownership and responsibility. All the important publics work together for the organization. Your unmanageable organization just got a whole lot easier to manage.

Of course, the downside is that publics do change and may not share the hard won mission and/or vision. That is tough to deal with. Be aware of this downside and understand that it can happen. Ignoring it will set you up for failure.

You have now created a vision and know where your organization is going. You have created a mission that provides the framework for getting to where you want to go. But where are you now?

Chapter 12

Key Result Areas and Objectives

You can't really determine if you are making progress toward your vision and mission unless you first establish some baseline information that will provide a starting point. In the example of a personal savings plan, the baseline was $0 in savings. The objectives built on that baseline to get to the stated goal. Each objective was rather simple and easily measured.

In organizations, goals and objectives may not be so simple to establish and the baseline information may be more difficult to come by. For your organization, it might be easier to use the term "Key Result Areas" rather than goals.

Key Result Areas are based on the Mission Statement. What are the key areas defined by your mission for which results should and can be measured? These key areas are either stated directly by the mission or inferred by it. In other words, there are some key areas that don't need to be stated exactly by the mission but are still necessary. Keep this in mind as we build these key result areas.

Let's consider the following Mission Statement:

To provide needed quality leisure activities and facilities for the community that are effective and efficient.

Based on this mission some Key Result Areas might be:

• Customer Satisfaction
• Team Building

- Community/Volunteer Partnerships
- Effective and Efficient Delivery of Service
- Effective and Efficient Use of Resources
- Marketing Plan
- Professional and Personal Growth
- Program Development and Enhancement

So where did these Key Result Areas come from? Remember that, as a good manager, you collected background information. You conducted surveys. You facilitated brainstorming sessions. All this information was used to create a mission statement. These ideas and information should not be thrown out after the mission statement is completed. Rather, these ideas and information are used to help develop Key Result Areas as well as other aspects of the Strategic Plan.

Objectives are measurable steps to achieve a Key Result Area. Objectives should contain four components:

- Quality Standards
- Performance Measures
- Who Measures & How Often
- Measurement Tools

There must be a standard by which we measure the Key Result Area. The performance measure must be established along with who does the measuring and how often. Finally, we must define the measurement tool. Without these components, there is no way to track progress, no one takes responsibility and we don't know how to measure the performance.

By establishing Key Result Areas with Objectives we have a tool for not only measuring where the organization is today but a tool for charting progress towards the organization's mission and vision.

Following are examples of Key Result Areas and Performance Measures:

Key Result Areas	Quality Standard
Customer Satisfaction	Clean facilities Safe facilities and programs Friendly and knowledgeable staff Quality experience Convenience of experience Well maintained parks and facilities Effective communication of information Appropriate appearance of staff
Team Building	Effective communication of information Problems solved by teams Projects managed by teams Recognition of team work
Community/Volunteer Partnerships	Seek new partnership opportunities Formalize e.g. contracts, agreements, etc. Ensure win-win relationship Recognize partnerships Provide/obtain partnership feedback
Efficient and Effective Delivery of Service	Measure service delivery
Efficient and Effective Use of Resources	Well maintained parks and facilities Clean facilities Safe facilities Resources inventoried Measure resources for effective use Measure resources for efficient use
Marketing Plan	Comprehensive for each area Obtain effectiveness feedback Obtain customer feedback
Professional & Personal Growth	Opportunities for training Opportunities for professional participation Appropriate rewards
Program Development and Enhancement	Programs meet community needs Programs based on current trends Safe programs Evaluate program life cycle

Customer Satisfaction

Quality Standard	Performance Measures	Who Measures/How Often	Measurement Tool
Clean facilities	90 % approval rating on customer comment card.	All Staff Frequency - 1 April - 1 Oct; min 10 card/week. 1 Oct - 1 April; min 2 card/week.	Customer Comment Card
Safe facilities and programs	90 % approval rating on customer comment card.	All Staff Frequency - 1 April - 1 Oct; min 10 card/week. 1 Oct - 1 April; min 2 card/week.	Customer Comment Card
Friendly and knowledgeable staff	90 % approval rating on customer comment card.	All Staff Frequency - 1 April - 1 Oct; min 10 card/week. 1 Oct - 1 April; min 2 card/week.	Customer Comment Card
Quality experience	90 % approval rating on customer comment card.	All Staff Frequency - 1 April - 1 Oct; min 10 card/week. 1 Oct - 1 April; min 2 card/week.	Customer Comment Card

Customer Satisfaction

Quality Standard	Performance Measures	Who Measures/How Often	Measurement Tool
Convenience of experience	90 % approval rating on customer comment card.	All Staff Frequency - 1 April - 1 Oct; min 10 card/week. 1 Oct - 1 April; min 2 card/week.	Customer Comment Card
Well maintained parks and facilities	90 % approval rating on customer comment card.	All Staff Frequency - 1 April - 1 Oct; min 10 card/week. 1 Oct - 1 April; min 2 card/week.	Customer Comment Card
Effective communication of information (internal and external)	90 % approval rating on customer comment card.	All Staff Frequency - 1 April - 1 Oct; min 10 card/week. 1 Oct - 1 April; min 2 card/week.	Customer Comment Card
Appropriate appearance of staff	90 % approval rating on customer comment card.	All Staff Frequency - 1 April - 1 Oct; min 10 card/week. 1 Oct - 1 April; min 2 card/week.	Customer Comment Card

Team Building

Quality Standard	Performance Measures	Who Measures	Measurement Tool
Effective communication of information	Employees score 90% or more on questionnaire of goals and objectives Employees score 90% or more on questionnaire of key policies	Supervisors	Goals and objective questionnaire Policy questionnaire
Problems solved by teams	50% of permanent staff participate in at least one division wide problem solving team 50% of permanent staff participate in at least one department wide problem solving team teams used to solve 75% of challenges	Supervisors	Team work score card
Projects managed by teams	50% of permanent staff participate in at least one division wide project team 50% of permanent staff participate in at least one department wide project team teams used to manage 75% of projects	Supervisors	Project management report
Recognition of team work	Recognition system in place	Division Head	Annual strategic plan report

Community/volunteer partnerships

Quality Standard	Performance Measures	Who Measures	Measurement Tool
Seek new partnership opportunities	Two new partnership opportunities explored by Dec 31 of each year.	Division head	Annual partnership report
Formalize contracts, agreements, etc.	100% of partnerships are formalized	Division head	Annual partnership report
Ensure win-win relationship	Each partnership identifies the benefits to each partner.	Division head	Contract, agreement or other formalized item
Recognize partnerships	Each partner receives written recognition at least annually	Division head	Annual partnership report
Provide/obtain partnership feedback	Partners rate the partnership as good or better on annual questionnaire	All staff	Partner satisfaction questionnaire

Efficient and effective delivery of service

Quality Standard	Performance Measures	Who Measures	Measurement Tool
Measure service delivery	100% of services identified for measurement are measured for efficiency 100% of services identified for measurement are measured for effectiveness	All staff	Activity Based Costing Flowchart

Efficient/effective use of resources

Quality Standard	Performance Measures	Who Measures	Measurement Tool
Well maintained parks and facilities	All parks and facilities maintained per maintenance guidelines All parks and facilities maintained efficiently	All staff	Maintenance guideline checklists Activity Based Costing
Clean facilities	All parks and facilities maintained per cleanliness guidelines All parks and facilities cleaned efficiently	All staff	Cleanliness checklists Activity Based Costing
Safe facilities	All parks and facilities maintained per safety guidelines All parks and facilities efficiently maintained for safety	All staff	Safety checklists Activity Based Costing
Resources inventoried	Annual resource inventory completed by 31 Dec each year	All staff	Annual inventory report
Measure resources for effective use	100% of identified resources are measured	All staff	Effectiveness measurement tool
Measure resources for efficient use	100% of identified resources are measured	All staff	Activity Based Costing

Professional & Personal Growth

Quality Standard	Performance Measures	Who Measures	Measurement Tool
Opportunities for training	Each employee provided with at least 4 training opportunities each year	Supervisors	Annual training report
Opportunities for professional participation	30% of staff provided an opportunity to belong to a professional organization or attend a professional meeting	Supervisors	Annual training report
Appropriate rewards	Reward/bonus system in place	Division head	Annual strategic planning report

Program Development and Enhancement

Quality Standard	Performance Measures	Who Measures	Measurement Tool
Programs meet community needs	90% of program offerings meet assessed community needs	Supervisors	Program services report
Programs based on current trends	75% of programs are based on current trends	Supervisors	Program services report
Safe programs	100% of programs are safe	Supervisors	Program safety assessment
Evaluate program life cycle	100% of programs evaluated for life cycle	Supervisors	Program life cycle evaluation

Marketing Plan

Quality Standard	Performance Measures	Who Measures	Measurement Tool
Comprehensive for each area	A comprehensive marketing plan is in place by ____	Division Head	Annual strategic plan report
Obtain Effectiveness Feedback	90% of customers questioned rate marketing as effective	Marketing Department	Marketing effectiveness questionnaire
Obtain Customer Feedback	90% of customers questioned rate marketing as good or better	Marketing Department	Marketing questionnaire

Some of the above examples use numerical performance measures. These numbers depend on established baselines modified by measuring the performance for a trail period. For example, one of the objectives for the key result area of Customer Satisfaction is Clean Facilities. You can't establish 90% approval rating until you know what the approval rating is right now (where you are today). Therefore you must use the measurement tool for a specific time, tally the results and determine where you are today. If the current approval rating is 50% you might set a Performance Measure at 60% for the first year and increase it year by year. Of course the percentage and time frame are variable but must be practical. Since it is constantly measured it can be adjusted if necessary. It is, however, more important to adjust the procedures to improve the approval rating rather than adjust the performance measure.

This might seem vague and a bit difficult but it does not have to be so. Ideally, you would like to have a 100% satisfaction rating on all your performance indicators. That is probably not practical. Someone will always complain about something. However, 80% or 90% is not all that hard to achieve and is a good rating to shoot for. If your current rating is very low, say 50%, then setting your performance objective at a lower level will give you success earlier and allow you to raise the bar sooner. It is easier to go from a rating of 50% to 60% than from 50% to 90%. You want to be at 90%, just make the steps smaller and keep progressing.

Chapter 13

Core Activities

Core activities are activities that consume the organization's resources. All organizational expenditures can be assigned to core activities. The majority of unmanageable organizations share three core activities. They are expressed through the organization's Key Result Areas. The three core activities are: Facility Care, Customer Care and (focus) Care. Focus care is the organization's focus. For a museum or Zoo the organization's focus is its collections. Therefore, the focus care for a museum or Zoo is Collection Care. Core activities are often found in an organization's mission statement, especially the organization's focus.

Customer Care

Customer care is absolutely the most important activity of any organization. Most unmanageable organizations have the general public as their customers. Your customers are those people who benefit from your mission. Providing customer service is more than just a thing an organization does, it requires a total commitment of the organization and its staff. If your staff does not understand the importance of customer care or they are not totally committed to it, you are faced with a key ingredient of an unmanageable organization.

Customer care is about paying attention to the smallest detail to satisfy the needs of your customer. A museum that has a great display of dinosaur artifacts with educational graphics can easily fail if that is all the customer care it offers. There is a specific set of human needs that must be met in an orderly fashion before the customer will be motivated to benefit from the dinosaur experience at the museum. These needs are identified in Maslow's Hierarchy of Needs:

- The physiological need.—This is basic human need that includes creature comforts such as rest rooms, food and water, heating and cooling, etc.
- The need for safety.—People need to feel safe in the environment you present to them.
- The need for belonging.—The atmosphere must be welcoming, friendly and accepting.

Once these three basic needs are met, your customer can then benefit from your organization's mission and meet their need for esteem and self-actualization. Too many organizations whose mission it is to educate or entertain or provide information fail to do so because they do not provide the three foundational human needs. These needs are in a hierarchy. They must be provided in order. One need builds on the one below it.

Unmanageable organizations often share in downplaying the importance of customer care. Many of the publics that support the organization believe the primary core activity of the organization should be the organizational focus activity. It is a huge challenge for the good manager to get all the publics to understand why the customer care core activity is primary and so important to the success of an organization. Many managers have lost this battle and found themselves without a job or trying to manage a failing organization.

I've know a number of Zoo Directors (managers) who struggled with convincing their publics that the first phase of a major facility upgrade should be a new visitor entrance, rest rooms, food and drink concessions, stroller rentals, etc. rather than a new building for the elephants. This upgrade is necessary to satisfy basic customer needs so they can enjoy the elephants and their exhibits.

A good manager must ensure the organization's publics are in agreement on the core activities of the organization and which one is primary. This is best done through the process of creating a vision and mission statement, establishing key result areas and the recognition of this fact:

An organization that does not make customer care its primary core activity will not meet its customers' basic needs and will not only be unmanageable but will eventually fail.

Facility Care

Every organization has some physical space and/or equipment that must be cared for. Even an organization that leases an office and all the equipment must care for the space and the equipment to maintain its value to the organization. For some organizations such as a museum or Zoo, facility care is a major activity that consumes the majority of the organization's resources.

Facility care may be as simple as sweeping the carpet once a week and emptying the trash daily. However, it also can be quite complex involving the establishment of preventive maintenance schedules for major building systems such as heating and cooling and hiring, training and supervising staff to carry out that maintenance. For whatever level of facility care your organization has, it is a core activity.

Organizational Focus Care

My experience is working in a Zoo. The organizational focus for a Zoo is its collections of plants and animals. Care of these collections is one of the major activities of the organization. A great many resources are allocated to care for these resources including staff, food, veterinary care, etc. While this organizational focus may be your organization's *raison d'etre*, it is not your primary activity. However, it is an extremely important activity requiring a knowledgeable staff and management.

The care provided this activity is clearly dependent on the organization's focus. While a Zoo's collection care may be quite extensive and complex another organization's care of its organizational focus may be limited and rather simple. Whatever the organizational focus, it is the one focus that benefits from a professional organization whose interests are the same. The American Museum Association is extremely important in providing guidance and support for a museum's focus care.

In addition, this area of focus care is often the one that attracts special oversight by government organizations. This oversight consists of inspections, audits, reports etc. to ensure compliance with standards that are created by law. While your organization may not involve government oversight, it would be a rare case indeed.

Chapter 14

Programs

It is often an advantage to subdivide a Core Activity into smaller units for the purpose of budgeting or reporting. Many organizations use program areas as a way to define a subdivision of the Core Activity. A program defines a specific activity within the Core Activity. For example, within the Core Activity of Customer Care, there may be an Education Program. Within the Core Activity of Collection Care, there may be a Conservation Program.

Program areas can be set up much like a small strategic plan. To be used for a budget, the program outline identifies goals, actions, activities and resources needed for the program area. It is not unusual for a governing authority to ask for budget cuts. Basing a budget on programs provides an effective way to show the effect of a budget cut when a program itself must be cut. In addition, defining program areas can provide a further means of tracking performance by narrowing the focus of the measurement tool. See the chapter on Measurement Tools for a tool to use in tracking programs.

Following is an example of a program area within the focus core activity of Collection Care:

Conservation Program

The conservation program is designed to help protect nature. This organization will actively support the conservation of endangered species populations and their natural ecosystems; promote "conservation aware-ness" in all programs and activities; give its highest priority to conserva-tion programming.

Goal—participate in captive (*ex situ*) programs

    action—provide the resources for 2 studbooks
    activity—Mandrill studbook
        a. resources needed
            100 hrs staff time
            $400 printing & postage
            computer hardware & software
        b. sources of resources
            organization budget
        c. action evaluation
            was the studbook published according to AZA guidelines
            was the studbook published within budget

    activity—Wild Asses studbook
        a. resources needed
            100 hrs staff time
            $300 printing & postage
            computer hardware & software
        b. sources of resources
            organization budget
        c. action evaluation
            was the studbook published according to AZA guidelines
            was the studbook published within budget

    action—provide the resources and become active participants of all
    Species Survival Plans for species held by the organization

activity—orangutan
- a. resources needed
    - 50 hrs staff time as management group member
    - $600 travel expenses
- b. sources of resources
    - organization staff
    - budget
- c. action evaluation
    - did staff participate in management group meetings
    - did participation meet budget limits
    - was information forwarded to management group in a timely fashion

activity—Lowland gorilla
- a. resources needed
    - 20 hrs staff time
- b. sources of resources
    - organization staff
- c. action evaluation
    - was information forwarded to management group in a timely fashion

activity—elephant
- a. resources needed
    - 20 hrs staff time
- b. sources of resources
    - organization staff
- c. action evaluation
    - was information forwarded to management group in a timely fashion

activity—Andean condor
    a. resources needed
        20 hrs staff time
    b. sources of resources
        organization staff
    c. action evaluation
        was information forwarded to management group in a timely fashion

activity—Asian small-clawed otter
    a. resources needed
        20 hrs staff time
    b. sources of resources
        organization staff
    c. action evaluation
        was information forwarded to management group in a timely fashion

activity—Asian wild horse
    a. resources needed
        50 hrs staff time as management group member
        $600 travel expenses
    b. sources of resources
        organization staff
        budget
    c. action evaluation
        did staff participate in management group meetings
        did participation meet budget limits
        was information forwarded to management group in a timely fashion

activity—cotton-top tamarin
    a. resources needed
        20 hrs staff time
    b. sources of resources
        organization staff
    c. action evaluation
        was information forwarded to management group in a timely fashion

activity—gibbon
    a. resources needed
        20 hrs staff time
    b. sources of resources
        organization staff
    c. action evaluation
        was information forwarded to management group in a timely fashion

activity—tree kangaroo
    a. resources needed
        20 hrs staff time
    b. sources of resources
        organization staff
    c. action evaluation
        was information forwarded to management group in a timely fashion

activity—Bali mynah
    a. resources needed
        20 hrs staff time
    b. sources of resources
        organization staff

c. action evaluation
was information forwarded to management group in a timely fashion

action—cooperate with other captive management programs as resources allow

activity-
a. resources needed
b. sources of resources
c. action evaluation

Goal—take part in wild (in situ) programs

action—provide resources to assist selected wildlife and wild places protection programs

activity—CBSG
a. resources needed
$300/yr
b. sources of resources
organization budget
c. action evaluation
did CBSG programs aid in conservation program

activity—National Park or reserve
a. resources needed
$1000/yr
surplus materials & supplies
b. sources of resources
private donations
organization surplus property

  c. action evaluation
     was the selected park appropriate to   vision
     did aid provide needed funds, material & supplies

action—assist with appropriate wildlife release programs and provide resources if necessary

  activity—American golden eagle
     a. resources needed
     b. sources of resources
     c. action evaluation

  activity—trumpeter swan
     a. resources needed
     b. sources of resources
     c. action evaluation

Goal—develop in-house programs that affect the way we work and the
way we live

  action—develop and implement a comprehensive recycling program
     a. resources needed
     b. sources of resources
     c. action evaluation

  action—evaluate operations to ensure efficient use of resources

     a. resources needed
        resource use committee
     b. sources of resources
        organization staff

   c. action evaluation
      was evaluation completed in appropriate time period
      were recommendations realistic and implemented

action—recommend life style changes to all staff that will help protect nature

activity—encourage use of mass transit and car pools
   a. resources needed
   b. sources of resources
   c. action evaluation

This program definition is very specific with goals that are set up for
the annual budget. It can also be used for not only program evaluation but
also staff evaluation. There may be a Director of Conservation in this
organization that must meet these program goals and/or track them.

The following example is a Facility Management program that falls
under the core activity of Facility Care. It is specific for the organization:

Facility Management Program

The organization will develop and manage all its facilities to meet the
needs of its staff, visitors and animal and plant collections. In addition, all
facilities will meet regulatory requirements. Animal facilities will provide
a comfortable and safe environment for the animal collection. Emphasis
of all animal facilities will be towards "home space", designing and managing space as the animal's home, and away from "exhibit space"/"holding
space". The plant collection will be developed and managed to enhance
the visitor's experience and impact the Organization in a positive way.

Goal—develop and manage all facilities to meet the needs of staff, visitors and the animal and plant collections

action—periodically evaluate the needs of facility users and recommend appropriate management changes

    a. resources needed
        40 hrs staff time/yr
    b. sources of resources
        organization staff
    c. action evaluation
        did evaluation occur at least annually

action—establish a list of facility enhancements, new support facilities and new animal facilities

    a. resources needed
        20 hrs staff time/yr
    b. sources of resources
        organization staff
    c. action evaluation
        was action accomplished

action—maintain a preventive maintenance program

    a. resources needed
        20 hrs per month staff time/yr
        $200 per month material & supplies
    b. sources of resources
        organization staff
        organization budget
    c. action evaluation
        were all PM items completed each month?
        were PM items completed within budget?

action—provide resources to maintain facilities in a safe, clean manner

> a. resources needed
>   budget equal to 5% of facility value
> b. sources of resources
>   organization budget
> c. action evaluation
>   were resources provided at adequate level?
>   were maintenance costs within projected levels?

Goal—manage all facilities to meet regulatory requirements

action—evaluate facilities and identify needs to meet regulatory requirements

> a. resources needed
>   20 hrs staff time/yr
> b. sources of resources
>   organization staff
> c. action evaluation
>   are regulatory requirements met

Goal—design and manage animal facilities as animal "homes"

action—design new animal facilities so that exhibit space is the space the animal lives in with shift space not used as an animal's home

> a. resources needed
>   staff time
> b. sources of resources
>   organization staff

    c. action evaluation
        was goal met for new facilities?

action—evaluate existing space for changes necessary to meet this goal

    a. resources needed
        staff time
    b. sources of resources
        organization staff
    c. action evaluation
        was goal met for existing facilities?

Programs can be a valuable way to focus your organization's Core Activities. It gives staff a more "down to earth" way of understanding the vision and mission of the organization. Additionally, programs give a great deal of detail that can be used not only in budgeting but also for individual and teamwork priorities and ways to measure progress on those priorities.

Chapter 15

Standards of Care

Each core activity must have a set of standards that address how each activity will be cared for. These standards:

- Provide your organization's publics with information that will show that you are caring for and protecting those things they are interested in.
- Provide staff with guidelines for their day-to-day work.
- Provide a basis for staff performance evaluations.
- Provide a basis for some of the organization's performance tools.
- Provide guidelines for carrying out key result areas of the organization.

Standards of care should include standards adopted by your parent or professional organization. There are many standards of care in the public domain for such things as lawn care, building care, equipment care, etc. Some standards may be developed in-house for specific or unique parts of your organization's activities.

Customer care standards must be a priority for the good manager. These standards must provide for the basic needs of the customer, define processes by which customers are served and determine guidelines for how staff interacts with customers.

Zoos and museums, among others, have the visiting public as a primary customer. These organizations market programs and activities to the visiting public to maintain or increase attendance. However, there is one element of customer care that I find lacking in many of these organizations. Studies have shown that visiting one of these institutions is mostly a family activity. We all know the schedule of the U.S. family: Monday through Friday–kids in school all day, adults at work all day; weekends–sports activities, church, shopping, house and lawn care. Many Zoos and museums and other public organizations are open to the visiting public, at best, seven days a week; 10:00 AM to 5:00 PM. Many close earlier. If you match up these schedules it should become clear that the only time a family can visit one of these institutions is during the day on <u>weekends</u>. That visit is in competition with numerous other activities. It is a wonder those institutions have any attendance at all! To further compound the problem, most staff members want weekends off. The fewest number of employees often staff the highest days of attendance.

Managers. Wake Up. You are providing poor customer care if you aren't even open when those customers are available to visit. You are providing poor customer care if the majority of your key staff is off when the majority of your customers visit. You cannot accomplish your mission, your focus core activity, without great customer care.

Unfortunately, unmanageable organizations do not allow managers to correct this problem and poor managers don't recognize it as a problem. Standards of care for customers should be written to incorporate the wants and needs of the customer with less regard for the wants and needs of the staff.

Following is a Standard of Care document for a rented office space:

<u>**Standards Of Care–Facility**</u>

XYZ occupies rented office space which must be cared by according to the standards listed in this document. These standards meet or exceed the requirements of the office space lease agreement with ABC Company.

Office Floors

A contracted janitor service will vacuum office floors covered with carpeting at least once per week. Carpeted floors will be shampooed or steam cleaned every 6 months by a contracted janitor service.

A contracted janitor service will sweep non-carpeted floors at least once per week. These floors will be striped and waxed every 6 months by a contracted janitor service.

Trash

Trashcans will be emptied and trash removed from the office premises daily by a contracted janitor service.

All recyclable paper, cans, bottles, etc. will be placed in appropriate recycle bins that will be picked up by a contracted recycling company at least weekly.

Compliance with standards

The Office Supervisor will be responsible for contracting with service companies and ensuring compliance with these facility standards.

Following is a Standard of Care document for a Zoo collection. This example[1] is complex due to the nature of the core activity and contains standards from professional organizations, government and the organization.

Standards Of Care—Collections

Quality standards for animal care will generally meet the standards set forth in the requirements for accreditation set by the American Zoo and Aquarium Association, in husbandry manuals developed for specific Species Survival Plans and regulations of Federal, State and Local governments. The standards in this document add, clarify and/or strengthen those of accreditation, SSPs and government agencies.

---

[1] The original draft of these standards was written by Ron Kaufman, former Education Director, Topeka Zoological Park.

Behavioral modification/enrichment

The Zoo recognizes the importance of enriching the lives of its animals by stimulating natural behaviors or recreating social living conditions. It also recognizes that sometimes some animal's behavior will need to be modified to render it more tractable for handling or care, to extinguish unsafe or undesirable behaviors, to reinforce natural behaviors, or to make it more likely to carry out parental responsibilities. These standards set those conditions under which staff and volunteers are allowed to modify and enrich behaviors, and by what means.

Collection Management will develop procedures whereby behavior modification projects will be reviewed before permission can be given to start them. A behavior modification project will be approved only if it is can be shown that it will benefit the welfare of the animal or its species, improve its care, or benefit the safety or other animals.

Acceptable behavioral modification reinforcements

- food, healthful snacks
- gentle praise
- stroking, if it can be done safely and if the animal seems to like it
- access to pleasant or desirable visual, auditory, tactile, social stimuli; e.g. searching for food, play items, curiosity items (zebra dung placed in lion exhibit)
- play with handler, if it can be done safely

Unacceptable reinforcements

- access to or administration of psychoactive or habit-forming substances
- sexual stimulation

Acceptable behavioral modification punishment

- stern voice
- withholding positive reinforcements

Unacceptable punishment

- electric shock
- striking with anything other than an open hand
- the standards of humane conduct will apply at all times

Water and Watering of the Animals

Frequency of watering

Each animal or exhibit containing animals will be provided with clean fresh drinking water at least once each day. In the event that outdoor temperatures cause the drinking water to freeze, the animal or exhibit will be provided with water at least twice during the day. Water for some species may be prevented from freezing by appropriate water heaters or other approved mechanisms.

Presentation

The watering vessels will be placed so that the animals they are intended for can easily reach them but are generally out of public view either by location or camouflage. The vessels will be positioned so as to discourage the animal from fouling the vessel with feces, urine or other wastes or debris. In the event the nature of the animal is such that they use the water as a pool or waste deposition site, then a separate vessel for drinking water will be provided which is designed or positioned to discourage the animal from using it as a pool or waste deposition site. In the event there is social competition for a drinking vessel, enough drinking vessels will be provided to accommodate subordinate animals, or action will be taken to modify the group dynamics to ensure that each animal is allowed to drink.

Watering vessels

Vessels for drinking water will be of a kind which can be easily cleaned and disinfected and will hold a minimum amount of water that is necessary for drinking. Large vessels which hold voluminous amounts of water are discouraged because their design discourages frequent cleaning, encourages waste of water, promotes the formation of mud if drained onto open ground, and present risks to personnel in trying to handle their weight. Vessels will be matched to the natural history of the animal for which they are intended, keeping in mind that some animals can drown in inappropriately designed or presented vessels. Shallow water vessels will be provided for those individuals that may be prone to drowning in deep vessels.

Cleaning

Drinking vessels will be drained and cleaned at least once each day and disinfected at least once weekly. In the event a drinking vessel is fouled with food, feces, urine, blood or other body excretions, the vessel will be cleaned and refilled with clean water when found to be fouled.

Exceptions

If, according to a veterinarian, an animal should not be given access to drinking water because of a health risk, then the animal will not be given access to water or be given water until such time as the veterinarian permits it.

The physical nature of the hippopotamus pool and the sheer size of the animal preclude the provision of a separate drinking water vessel. However, the pool in which the animals live will be cleaned and refilled with fresh water daily.

Other habitat areas housing aquatic or semi-aquatic animals need not have a separate drinking vessel but those water areas will be cleaned according to a prescribed schedule.

Animals (principally water birds) that live on open water will not be given separate drinking water, unless the water is found to have frozen completely and no open water is available.

Amphibians are sensitive to the quality of water. They will be provided with water that is cleanly aged, distilled or chemically neutralized. Their water can be provided environmentally by sprinkling it around their habitat, if their nature is such to require such actions.

Fishes, totally aquatic reptiles or totally aquatic amphibians need not be provided separate drinking opportunities other than their environmental pools.

Foods And Feeding

Quality statement: Animals offered vegetable and fruit foodstuffs will be offered only such foodstuffs which are of the quality no less than food normally consumed by the animal in the wild. No animal will be fed spoiled, moldy, tainted, or otherwise fouled foodstuffs. The Zoo will not accept donations of meat or eggs salvaged from freezers or refrigerators that have malfunctioned. No animal will be fed foodstuffs tainted with vermin feces, urine, hair or bodies, provided that some acceptable levels may exist in processed foods as determined by USDA regulations.

Storage of food

Perishable fruits and vegetables will be kept refrigerated until they are prepared for use. Those not requiring refrigeration will be kept in vermin-proof containers. Moldy fruits and vegetables in a batch will be discarded when found. Arriving shipments will be inspected for evidence of poor quality and the damaged portions will be returned to the vendor.

Dry feeds will be kept in vermin-proof containers, or stored in sacks in vermin-proof containers or buildings.

Meat products will be kept frozen or refrigerated until use. Frozen meat products will be thawed in a refrigerator until they are prepared for feeding. Thawed meat or meat products will not be re-frozen for later use.

Live food that is killed before feeding must either be fed within one hour of being killed or be frozen or refrigerated until such time as it is needed utilizing a plate or similar to protect preparation surfaces from contamination.

Refrigerated meat products, whole animals, eggs or egg products will be refrigerated for no more than seven days.

Food dishes that are prepared for distribution to animals and that contain perishable or meat products must be kept refrigerated until just before they are distributed. Such dishes must be presented within 30 minutes of removal from refrigeration.

Handling

Persons preparing foodstuffs for animals will wash their hands prior to beginning such preparation. Preparers will wash their hands each time after they handle meat or raw egg products before subsequently handling fruits, vegetables or dry feeds. Preparers may elect to use disposable gloves for food preparation and clean up. Utensils used to prepare meat or egg products will be washed before using the same utensils to prepare fruits and vegetables.

Food preparers will wash their hands before handling live animals after they have prepared foods.

Work surfaces on which meat products or killed animals were prepared will be thoroughly cleaned and disinfected before using the same surface for preparing fruits and vegetables or dry feeds.

Food preparation surfaces will be thoroughly cleaned after the preparation session is complete and disinfected at the end of the day, and all utensils used for preparation will likewise be thoroughly cleaned after use.

Preparation

Meals for the animals will be prepared according to the instructions on the animal's diet card. Deviations and substitutions will be allowed only after approval from Collection Management.

Presentation

The food or feeding vessels will be placed so that the animals for which they are intended can easily reach them and will be presented in a manner that is appropriate to the animal's natural feeding styles. The food or vessel will be positioned so as to discourage the animal from fouling it with feces, urine or other wastes or debris. In the event there is social competition for food, enough food or vessels will be provided to accommodate subordinate animals, or action will be taken to modify the group dynamics to ensure that each animal is allowed to eat. If necessary, some animals will be removed from others to ensure them their proper allotment of food. Food will not be left available for an animal to consume for longer than 24 hours. It will be removed immediately if spoiled, moldy or otherwise unfit for consumption or if conditions are such that it is likely to spoil before the 24-hour limit. Food dishes presented to on-exhibit animals will be shielded from public view wherever possible.

Food will be presented to the animal in a location comparable to the location it might be found in the natural habitat.

Cleaning

Feeding vessels will be cleaned after pickup and disinfected daily. In the event an animal has not yet eaten but has fouled its food with dirty water, feces, urine, blood or other body excretions, the vessel will be cleaned and refilled with clean food when found to be soiled.

Browse

Some animals will be given browse as a means to stimulate activity, enrich their time or to augment natural feeding or browsing behavior. The browse will consist of parts of shrubbery, trees or other plants that are known to be harmless to the species to which they are offered. The browse may be collected from specimens on the Zoo grounds, harvested from the Tropical Rain Forest or provided by other means as approved by Collection Management. Browse may be cleaned and sanitized with diluted chlorine upon recommendation of the Zoo Veterinarian.

Exceptions

If, according to a veterinarian, an animal should not be given access to food because of a health risk, then the animal will not be given access to food or be given food until such time as the veterinarian permits it.

Origin of foodstuffs

Zoo animals will be fed from only those foods provided to the staff for diet preparation, or from an approved list of browse. Staff will not offer any other food, snack or treat items to animals without permission of Collection Management.

Hay Quality and presentation

Hay will be inspected prior to feeding for the presence of contaminants such as glass, wire, nails, trash, poisonous plants, mold, etc. If such contaminants are found, they will be removed before the hay is fed. If they cannot be removed, then the bale will be discarded and another bale of hay will be selected. In all cases, hay will be removed from its baling twine or wire before being fed. Hay fed outdoors will be dispensed only from off-the-dirt feeders or platforms. Hay used indoors, on cleanable concrete floors, may be fed directly from the floor, if it can be protected from contamination. Hay should be fed at the level the animal would normally find browse or graze in its natural habitat.

Nutritional analysis of all hays must be within 20% of the established norms as reported in the Feeds Database of the Animal Nutritionist Program. Hay will be analyzed when acquired and stored hay will be tested every 4-6 months. Hay, especially alfalfa, that have stems comprising 50% or more of any bale should not be fed. Hay stored over two years should not be fed unless permitted by Collection Management.

Public Feeding

Public feeding of the animals will be discouraged except of the ducks, geese, swans, if done with Zoo supplied food; or at the Zoo contact area, if done under supervision of staff, using Zoo supplied food.

Habitat Standards

The habitat of the animal is the place where the animal lives. The Zoo will present each animal and its habitat in a way that approximates the natural habitat represented by using the latest technology and construction techniques while maintaining proper security. Further, the habitat and its furnishings will be managed and designed so each species' natural behaviors can be expressed. Behaviors that do not lend themselves to the Zoo environment will be limited by design and/or managed as prescribed by Collection Management.

Species to be represented in the Zoo's collection will be defined in the Institution Collection Plan. This plan will recommend species to be held by the Zoo based on appropriateness of facilities, resources for adequate care, and compliance with Master Plan projects, conservation priority and availability.

Species with outside habitats will be allowed to live in those habitats at least 23 hours per day except under certain weather, maintenance or veterinary related conditions. However, any time not spent in outdoor habitats will be considered less than the "best care possible" for the species.

Holding space is provided where animals may be placed:

- while the habitat is being cleaned or otherwise maintained
- upon the order of the Zoo Veterinarian due to quarantine or treatment
- to prepare animals for shipment
- to prevent injury to the animal due to behavioral problems.

Animals will not be held in a holding situation for longer than 30 days. Longer holding periods will be considered as not meeting proper standards of care.

Indoor habitats will provide animals with the necessary light spectrum and proper light cycles if natural sunlight is not available. Indoor habitats will provide the proper humidity, heating and cooling necessary to maintain near natural habitat conditions. Each indoor habitat will have posted the range of acceptable levels of light, lighting cycles (if natural sunlight is not available), humidity and temperature for the animals living in them. Mechanical devices will be installed to ensure compliance with the range of acceptable environmental conditions.

Staff will take all steps necessary to limit visitor viewing of service areas especially from habitat viewing areas. Exceptions may be made for "behind the scenes" tours as identified by Collection Management.

Habitat Furnishings

The Zoo emphasizes the importance of providing furnishings in a habitat to provide the animal a sense of security, offer a variety of play or locomotion opportunities, and stimulate healthful activity. Recognizing that the Zoo also has a duty to accurately represent an animal's natural history, it is also important that such furnishings complement the animal, its habitat, natural history and behavior.

Acceptable furnishings

These standards recognize the difference between on-exhibit and off-exhibit animals for aesthetic applications. Furnishings for on-exhibit animal habitats will be held to a higher cosmetic standard than those in off-exhibit habitats. In all cases, furnishings will be securely anchored to prevent accidental falls under the animal or on top of the animal, excessive movement by the animals, accidental hangings and strangulations or use as escape devices, weapons, or habitat-damaging objects. They will be anchored without protruding nails, exposed wire ends, screws, bolts, etc. that could cause injury to the animals.

Ropes, hoses, vines, cords, and chains will be draped and anchored so as to prevent twists or loops that may accidentally strangle an animal. Nooses will not be permitted. Chains and heavy hoses will be anchored at both ends.

Branches, logs, twigs, and stumps will be securely anchored. They will be of sufficient strength so as not to collapse under the weight of the animal. They will be placed and arranged in such a manner that they cannot be used as escape devices or routes.

Rocks will be arranged so as to discourage animals from moving them. Stacked rocks will be arranged and/or anchored so that an animal cannot become pinned beneath them. Generally, in a stacked or piled rock arrangement, the larger, heavier rocks will be on the bottom, the smaller, lighter rocks on the top. Maintenance staff or those persons knowledgeable in masonry techniques will construct rock shelters. Support walls of a rock shelter will be constructed with mortar or concrete if numerous small rocks are used to support a rock slab roof. Collection Management and the facility supervisor will determine if such construction techniques are necessary.

Live plants will be used which are not poisonous to the species for which they are used. Any live plant that can be targeted by an animal as food will be protected from predation in a manner that is unobtrusive (unless the plant is intended to be used for food). Care will be exercised to make sure the plant cannot be bent, toppled or otherwise adapted into an escape route or device.

Artificial representations of trees or rocks will be designed and fabricated to withstand the onslaught of everyday use and abuse by the animal and the prevailing climate. They will be installed in such a manner that they cannot be loosened, and so that an animal cannot crawl into the supporting armature. Exposed glass fabric or strands will not be allowed on finished fiberglass representations.

Paints will consist of nontoxic latex paints or hard epoxy enamels anywhere that an animal may attempt to lick, consume, rub off or scratches off the paint. Lead-based paints will not be used.

Plastic or fabric plants will be used sparingly within an exhibit and not at all if it is likely the animal will attempt to consume them. They can be used more freely if placed out of reach of an animal and in subdued light or at a distance from the viewing public.

Accurate representations

Wherever an on-exhibit animal habitat is being furnished, the furnishings will be natural or natural-appearing wherever practical. The use of furnishings normally made by people for people use will not be allowed, unless the exhibit is intended to convey a message of animal/human interaction or human impact on the animal. These standards recognize the practical restrictions of furnishing a habitat for such large animals as elephants, hippos, horses, camels, giraffes or bears. Nevertheless, a natural appearing habitat will always be a goal, if not an immediate reality.

On-exhibit habitats, which attempt to recreate the look of a wild habitat, will be furnished to accurately represent the natural habitat and habits of the animal that is on display. The furnishings will also be in keeping with any established habitat theme as determined by the Zoo for education, conservation, recreation or research purposes.

Non-acceptable furnishings

There are some furnishings which by their nature are detrimental to the health and safety of an animal or do not complement the naturalistic goals of habitats. They include: known toxic plants, rocks or logs that can be rolled or pushed about freely (unless intended for toys), unnatural artifacts such as pop bottles, cans, etc.

Habitat Cleanliness

Recognizing that maintaining clean, safe habitats for our animals is one of the best means for controlling disease, injury, pests, odors and public disdain, the Zoo will follow these standards of habitat cleanliness.

<u>Cleaning procedure</u>

This will be the generally followed cleaning procedure where a surface can be hosed and scrubbed:

- remove soiled bedding, old hay, food and feces with shovels, rakes, or brooms or squeegees
- rinse with water
- apply an approved detergent
- scrub or mop with the detergent
- rinse away the spent detergent
- apply the approved disinfectant and spread with hose or brush
- allow the disinfectant to stand for the prescribed amount of time or scrub with the disinfectant for the prescribed time
- rinse thoroughly
- allow the surface to dry or squeegee dry before reapplying bedding or returning the animal

Animals will be removed from the area being cleaned to prevent them from being sprayed with water, chemicals or debris.

"Spot cleaning," where the soiled bedding is removed and the floor broomed or squeegeed, followed by reapplication of clean bedding, will be allowed if the habitat is such that less than daily total cleaning is prescribed. Otherwise "spot cleaning" can be applied only once in a 48 hour period. Those habitats will be "spot cleaned" one day and "wet cleaned" the following day.

Collection Management will prescribe the types, quantities and usage of various detergents and disinfectants.

This will be the generally followed cleaning procedure where a surface is composed of loose soil, sand or other "natural" substrate:

- spot clean the debris with shovels, rakes, spoons or paper towels
- remove damp and/or odorous substrates down to exhibit floor, where it occurs replace with a clean substrate
- in the event there is a persistent odor of ammonia, an enclosed exhibit will be cleaned by changing the substrate and cleaning furnishings.
- outdoor yards and exhibits will be cleaned following step one above, but in the case of persistent odor, disease problem, or pest infestation the other steps may be employed to help ensure animal health.

Enclosures containing animals will be cleaned at least once daily. The furnishings of exhibits containing animals that scent-mark their territory will be cleaned as needed to control pests and odors, but will not be cleaned daily.

Enclosures where the debris falls onto papers below the cage floor will have their papers changed daily.

The area around animal enclosures will be kept clean and free of debris, including but not limited to hair, feathers, old food, trash, and soiled bedding.

Discarded bedding, exhibit debris, old food, feces, etc. will be disposed of in the manner prescribed by Collection Management.

Tools and equipment used in cleaning procedures will be cleaned after each use. No piece of equipment or tool used in cleaning will be allowed to sit overnight without itself being cleaned.

Drain catch baskets and drain covers (soiled after a habitat is cleaned) will be cleaned at the end of the cleaning procedure.

Use of chemicals

Staff will use only those cleaning chemicals that have been provided for their use and will use them according to manufactures' recommendations unless Collection Management sets a different protocol.

Quarantine/cross-contamination

The veterinarian can elect to quarantine an animal in its habitat, rather than in isolation. In all cases where an animal is quarantined, staff will follow the veterinarian's instructions for cleaning the habitat, tools and other equipment and will use any footbath, disinfectant soaks or personal health-protection devices that are provided.

Standing water/mud

Unless providing for the health or behavior of an animal, staff will attempt to eliminate persistent standing water and mud in animal habitats. These standards recognize that after rains or snow melt some temporary standing water is to be expected.

Bedding

Animals that can be bedded will be given bedding material, as determined by Collection Management. The bedding will be that provided for that purpose and in all cases it will be clean and free of debris.

Habitat Climate Control

Climate may fluctuate greatly on a seasonal basis. It may be necessary to climate control animal habitats. The acceptable temperature and humidity levels will be set by Collection Management and will be adhered to as best as possible within the boundaries of sound equipment function.

In the event of equipment failure where an animal is exposed to unacceptable temperature or humidity levels, the animal will be removed from the area or an alternate means of climate control will be provided.

Any climate control equipment or its parts, whether heater, fan, air conditioner, heating pad or vents will be kept out of the reach of the animal and the animal will not be allowed to climb on, crawl under or get into any such equipment.

Forced air movement will be directed so that an animal is not exposed to chilling drafts or overly hot, drying drafts.

Habitat Maintenance

Repair scene management

The facility supervisor will be responsible for directing maintenance workers at the scene of a repair. Animal care staff will advise maintenance workers on the safe distance beyond which to keep equipment, tools and materials. Animal care staff will be responsible for moving and securing animals away from the repair scene, if necessary, and for providing protection to maintenance workers when an animal cannot be removed from the scene.

Inspections, obstructions and protrusions

Animal care staff will frequently examine animal habitats to check for protruding wires, broken glass, loose screws and bolts, faulty locks and latches, compromised barriers or other such mechanical or physical abnormality which could endanger the health or safety of the animals, staff or public. If such a situation is found, action to safeguard animal and human safety will be taken immediately.

Repair scene cleanup

Maintenance workers will remove all debris, tools, equipment and materials from the habitat after their work is finished. Animal care staff will further inspect and clean the habitat of any remaining debris, chemicals or foreign objects prior to allowing the animal to return to the habitat.

Liquid substances

Liquid maintenance or cleaning substances will be thoroughly removed or flushed away from the habitat after a maintenance procedure and drain baskets, drains, and cleaning tools will be cleaned as well. Liquid maintenance chemicals will be stored according to manufacturers' recommendations away from animal habitats and beyond the reach of animals. Animal watering vessels, feeding dishes and implements used to prepare animal food will not be used to hold, dispense or store anything other than drinking water or food.

Pest Control

The Zoo recognizes the need for effective and persistent pest control measures to help assure good animal health, promote a sound physical plant and to present a good image to our visitors. The veterinarian will be broadly responsible for establishing pest control procedures and for providing appropriate and safe chemical or mechanical means to control pests. Whenever possible, non-toxic methods will be employed to control pests.

Cleanliness

Service areas, areas around habitats and areas where trash and garbage is discarded will be kept clean and neat.

Disposal of manure and garbage

Manure, garbage, soiled bedding and trash will be discarded in the manner and by the means established by Collection Management.

Use of chemicals/application

Pest control chemicals, treatments and equipment will be prepared and applied in accordance with manufacturers' recommendations unless directed otherwise by Collection Management. Personal health protection equipment, OSHA approved, will be provided and used to help ensure safe application of pest control measures.

Equipment

Pest control equipment will be used in accordance with manufacturers' recommendations and will be cleansed in the manner recommended by manufacturer or Collection Management.

Unused chemicals/storage

Pest control chemicals and treatments will be kept stored away from contact by animals in the manner recommended by manufacturer or Collection Management. Such chemicals will not be stored in, mixed in or dispensed from any implement used to prepare or dispense animal or human drinking water or food. Used or spent chemicals will be discarded in accordance with manufacturers' recommendations and/or as directed by local hazardous materials disposal guidelines.

Acceptable methods for controlling pests and for disposing of live-trapped mammalian or avian pests

- commercially available poisons
- traps; live, snap, box
- flushing burrow
- burying burrow

Unacceptable methods for controlling mammalian or avian pests

- gasoline
- fire

Veterinary Care

Authority for veterinary care

A licensed veterinarian has the sole authority to diagnose, order tests, prescribe treatments and manage the treatment of an animal's disease, injury or other health matters. The veterinarian will establish and maintain a preventive medicine program, clinical diagnosis and treatment program, a pathology program and a medical records program.

Restrictions on applications of treatments

Other staff will be allowed to dispense and administer medications and treatments only if such medications and treatments are prescribed by the veterinarian and only upon written instructions to do so from the veterinarian. Collection Management may transmit instructions from the veterinarian, but only the veterinarian will provide written instructions for those staff being directed to administer such medications or treatments. Volunteers will not administer any medications.

Veterinary emergencies

The veterinarian will provide standing orders and/or set protocol for handling emergencies in his or her absence. Such emergency privileges will be given only to those persons designated by the veterinarian and only after those persons have been trained to implement said orders and protocol.

Medically restricted access

The veterinarian, upon consultation with Collection Management team, may designate certain areas as "Medically Restricted." All nonhuman primate areas are deemed as "Medically Restricted." Only persons who have tested negative within one year for tuberculosis on the basis of a skin test or chest X-ray will be allowed in those areas. Further, any such persons must also be free of all of the following diseases: measles, mumps, rubella, chicken pox, influenza, tuberculosis, or any other contagious disease as determined by the veterinarian. Only those people who meet the above qualifications will be allowed direct contact with any nonhuman primate kept at the Zoo. Exceptions may be granted by Collection Management if an emergency exists, if there is need for non-staff maintenance personnel access to the area, or if there is a greater risk to the animal's health posed by denying a person's access than the risk posed by the possibility of disease.

Immobilization/scene conduct

Only a licensed veterinarian will be allowed to perform or supervise a chemically induced restraint, immobilization or anesthesia procedure, unless an emergency exists.

The veterinarian will be responsible for assigning tasks to assisting personnel and will direct the course of the procedure. If the procedure is part of a larger event, such as a transport, the Collection Management team will direct support personnel in cooperation with the veterinarian to ensure a safe and efficient event for the animal, supporting persons and the public.

Any capture, restraint, immobilization or anesthesia whether by physical or chemical means will be planned and conducted with the safety and welfare of the animal, staff and public in mind. Generally, animal care staff is responsible for physical capture and physical restraint.

Any staff on the scene of a capture, physical or chemical restraint, immobilization or anesthesia will conduct themselves in a quiet and efficient manner, without horseplay, loud noises or loud conversation and with utmost regard for the safety and welfare of the animal, other staff and the public. Persons entering the area or non-staff observing will be directed to behave in a like manner. Animals under the effects of a restraining chemical will not be talked to or subjected to shouts, loud noises, slaps, prods or similar actions unless such action is directed by a veterinarian to determine the level of effect.

Humane application of veterinary care

Any veterinarian attending a Zoo animal will perform their duties according to such humane guidelines as may be established by the veterinary profession. Further, an animal under a chemical or physical restraint or immobilization that has no anesthetic effects will not be subjected to surgical procedures unless the site is anesthetized locally or regionally or unless the animal is given a general anesthetic.

Euthanasia

Only a licensed veterinarian will perform elective euthanasia, except of food animals, in which case another staff member may perform the procedure, following written instructions from the veterinarian. Volunteers will not perform any euthanasia. Euthanasia can be considered for any of the following reasons: severe and irreparable injury, severe or chronic illness where the prognosis for recovery is doubtful, severe congenital defects at birth, conditions that prevent the animal from maintaining a good quality of life, postnatal rejection where hand-rearing will be required but is undesirable or impractical.

Any elective euthanasia will be performed according to the guidelines of the American Veterinary Medical Association. The Zoo Director will develop the procedures to review and act on any proposed elective euthanasia and will have final authority for such action.

Emergency euthanasia can be performed by a licensed veterinarian or Zoo administrative official (using standing orders dispensed by a veterinarian) at their discretion, if there is overwhelming evidence of a likely untreatable injury or sudden illness accompanied by signs of extreme pain or if a situation exists where an animal is threatening the life of or is likely to cause permanent debilitating injury to a member of the staff or public (as in an animal escape or human suicide attempt).

Any euthanasia will be followed by the completion of such forms and reports as may be required by law or administrative procedure.

Quarantine

Animals which are newly acquired by means other than birth or hatching within the Zoo collection or those determined to have or likely to have a disease contagious to other animals will be quarantined for a length of time to be set by a licensed veterinarian. The veterinarian in cooperation with Collection Management will also set the location in the Zoo for such quarantine.

Animals brought to the Zoo by the public for identification or release will not be taken into any animal habitat or animal building, but will remain in non animal office areas or outdoors.

Equipment, tools and personal gear used for the care of quarantined animals will be cleaned and used in a manner as prescribed by the veterinarian and as described previously.

Necropsy and disposition of carcasses/body parts

The Zoo recognizes the importance of postmortem examinations on animals to help determine cause of death, retrieve important research data and learn more about its anatomy and physiology.

Only a licensed veterinarian, who also has sole authority to determine and state a cause of death, will perform necropsies. A necropsy will be performed on all deceased animals unless the carcass is decomposed or consumed so much as to render necropsy data useless.

The proper disposition of carcasses and parts is the responsibility of the veterinarian or a designate and will be carried out according to the mandates of local laws, regulations or public health guidelines. Animal carcasses or parts thereof will not be disposed of in any public trash can and will not be placed in the Zoo dumpster unless first tightly enclosed in an opaque plastic trash bag.

Animal carcasses or parts being transported to an animal burial site, anywhere off the grounds, or to anywhere within the Zoo will be shielded from public view by opaque tarps, plastic sheeting, bags or drapes. Further, efforts will be made to contain dripping fluids. Large animals that expire on-exhibit and cannot quickly be moved out of public view will likewise be covered until they can be removed. Requests from visitors to "peek" at the carcass will not be granted.

The veterinarian will keep a record of requests of body parts for legitimate research purposes and will attempt to meet such requests where practical.

Carcasses or body parts/products salvaged from any deceased or living Zoo animal will not be allowed to enter private possession, including but not limited to those of endangered, threatened or vulnerable species. If the Zoo for education or research cannot use such parts, then they can be offered to other Zoos, museums or similar institutions, or they will be discarded. Disposition of eagles, their parts, nests and eggs and any other species and their parts that fall under Federal law will be disposed of according to the law.

Injured and orphaned wildlife

The Zoo frequently receives requests for help from people who have come to possess an injured or orphaned animal. These standards will direct that injured wildlife brought to the Zoo receive veterinary attention if available, or that the owner is referred to a private veterinarian, if the veterinarian is not available. The appropriate authorities will be notified in those cases where the species falls under the protection of law or regulation. Collection Management will develop specific protocols for dealing with orphaned or injured wild animals that are brought to the Zoo.

Do Not Resuscitate/Denial of Life saving Care

The veterinarian can, upon consultation with Collection Management, declare a sick or injured animal so sick that death is inevitable and that resuscitation measures would be without merit and should not be performed. Likewise, the veterinarian can, upon consultation with Collection Management, deny life saving medications and/or procedures to a sick or injured animal, but must either euthanize the animal or provide those medications and procedures that will reduce or eliminate pain. In all cases, the animal will be provided food and water, be assisted to eat if necessary and will be subject to the same standards of cleanliness as other animals.

Humane behavior toward the animals

The Zoo recognizes how important it is for all of its staff and volunteers to behave in a humane way toward its animals. The Zoo represents the "community conscience" for animal care and its personnel must be held to a high standard of humane conduct.

Teasing or goading

Animals will not be teased or goaded by anyone into displays of aggressive, submissive, fright or flight behavior for the benefit or anyone's entertainment or amusement. Animals will not be physically or mentally abused through the use of noises, prodding, striking, close confinement of long duration, isolation from normal and natural stimuli, throwing of objects, prolonged hosing, or spraying or feeding of obnoxious substances. Directing or shooting a BB gun, pellet gun, firearm or air pistol at an animal will not be allowed, except for such instruments that may be used to deliver drugs from a distance, or when the use of firearms is necessary to protect human life and welfare. Staff and volunteers will be held to broad interpretations of this section in order to protect the welfare of the animals.

Staff observing inhumane behaviors in other staff, visitors, guests or volunteers will be encouraged to intervene to stop such behavior, if such intervention can be done safely. If necessary, police officers will be called to assist.

Striking/prodding and "discipline"

These standards recognize that it occasionally may be necessary to strike or prod an animal to encourage it to move in a needed direction, to protect oneself from attack, to stop fighting among animals, to offer a "punishment" during behavior modification, or to test its responsiveness if ill or sedated. Other reasons may also surface. Nevertheless, some restraint is necessary to protect the welfare of the animal and to discourage wanton disregard for behavioral modification principles. Animals will not be struck on the head. Prods will be blunt and will be used to push or guide. At no time will the entry of a body orifice be allowed. Prodding and striking will be allowed only on the legs, back, shoulders, and rump. Forceful hosing of an animal's face, eyes, ears, nose, mouth, anus, vagina or penis will not be allowed. Drinking water being directly dispensed from a hose into the animal's mouth will have a gentle stream. Hurling objects such as sticks, rocks, sand or trash at an animal will not be allowed. Food or water will not be withheld for punishment purposes. Staff will be encouraged to seek alternate methods of inducing animals to move, to test responsiveness or to stop fighting.

Chordate food animals will be humanely killed, before being fed to another animal, except when the consuming animal will not eat killed food. In that case, every attempt will be made to convert the consumer to killed food animals as quickly as possible.

Elephants are managed under "protected contact" system. The Elephant Management Committee and Collection Management set guidelines for training and care. In general, behaviors are solicited verbally and rewarded. No person is permitted to be in an enclosure with an unrestrained elephant.

Staff and volunteers under the threat of death or permanently debilitating injury because of an animal attack will be allowed to do whatever is necessary to protect themselves. Likewise, those who are the victim of such an attack or respond to a situation where an attack is imminent will be allowed to pursue whatever means are necessary to stop the attack. In these instances, "whatever is necessary" can include the possibility of killing the attacking animal.

Security

The Zoo recognizes its responsibility to protect the safety and welfare of the animals it cares for, the staff that works here and the people who visit or live in the surrounding area.

Securing and locking habitats and containers

Staff will at all times use whatever mechanisms are provided to close, secure and lock entry into animal habitats whether occupied or not to prevent entry by unauthorized persons or to prevent escape by the animal. Entry doors into service areas, offices, and storage areas will be closed and locked as directed by Collection Management. Doors and gates will be locked at all times that lead to service space into which access by unauthorized persons could lead to physical contact with any animal unless staff is in the space and can monitor access by unauthorized persons.

Containers used to transport animals within the Zoo and for outreach activities will be closed and secured during the transport. If such container has a lock, the lock will be locked.

No one will be allowed to open the entry to or to enter a space that at the same time contains elephants or a member of the Felidae, Ursidae, Hyenidae, or Canidae families, unless exception is granted by Collection Management.

Alarms

Alarms will be kept in good working order, and will be tested and used as directed by Collection Management.

Non-staff personnel in service areas

Staff must accompany non-staff personnel in service areas, unless such personnel are volunteers or workers who have been instructed by staff on safe conduct in the areas. Former staff members, staff family and friends will be allowed into service areas after host staff notifies Collection Management and only if such guest is accompanied by current staff. Host staff of any guest, volunteer or worker will use discretion and prudence when permitting such persons to physically contact animals in service areas.

Escapes

Collection Management will develop the specific response procedures to animal escapes outside this document. However, these standards will direct that any response to an escape is predicated on consideration first for the safety of the public and staff and then of the animal. Further, those responding to an escape will permit the use of deadly force to control a dangerous animal if such action is warranted by the situation.

Transferring dangerous animals away from work areas

Staff will transfer dangerous animals into secure and lockable holding facilities before entering the animal's principal habitat. Staff will thoroughly inspect such "empty" habitats each and every time before entering and will close and lock same upon leaving. Collection Management will determine which animals will fall under authority of this section.

Record-keeping/Reporting

The Zoo recognizes the importance of maintaining accurate and timely records of matters pertaining to the collection. Collection Management will establish and maintain a collection record keeping system. The system will be able to coordinate with International Species Information System based data management systems. Further, a system of reporting needs for habitat maintenance and veterinary care to the appropriate persons will be maintained.

Animal data will be recorded in a succinct, objective and scientific manner and will include all the information required by Collection Management for maintaining useful and accurate records.

Interpretation of animals and their use in education.

The Zoo recognizes its mission to educate the community about wildlife and nature. It also recognizes that the animals are the most important ambassadors in such a mission. These standards set the criteria by which animals can be used in education programs and set the goals for their interpretation to our visitors.

Animal Handling Guidelines

Occasionally, it will be necessary to remove an animal from its display or from its holding quarters for an educational activity. Removal for such purposes is allowed by trained staff or trained volunteers under the following guideline:

- the removal will not constitute a hazard to the health and safety of the animal
- the removal will not constitute a danger to the public health and safety
- the removal will be coordinated with the animal's keeper
- the animal can be easily handled and restrained by one trained person
- the animal will be transported in an appropriate container and will not be allowed to roam freely in a vehicle during transport.

Members of the audience can be allowed to touch the animal, at the discretion of the handler, under the following guidelines:

- the touching will not constitute a hazard to the health and safety of the animals as determined in part by the size and character of the audience, and by the disposition of the animal
- the touching will not constitute a hazard to the health and safety of the audience
- the animal will remain under the control of the handler at all times
- the handler will arrange for a quiet and orderly format in which the touching will occur
- the audience will be instructed in the proper way to touch the animal
- the audience will be instructed in proper hygiene associated with animal handling

Interpretation

Animals on exhibit will be identified and interpreted by a label or larger graphic, except in those exhibits where the free-ranging animals can be difficult to find and where the theme stresses the habitat and not individual species. For example, many newer exhibits "immerse" the visitor in the exhibit. One enters the animals' habitat. A wide variety of animals may be present and the experience is of the habitat not the individual animal.

Animals will be correctly identified and all information offered will be accurate and timely. Written and verbal interpretation will respect the dignity of the animals, and will emphasize conservation issues where appropriate.

Weather

The Zoo recognizes its responsibility to protect its animals from weather extremes. Animals that cannot be adequately sheltered from weather will be moved elsewhere in the Zoo, or a shelter will be constructed, or the animals will be placed in other institutions that can handle their needs.

Shelter

The Zoo will provide shelter to each of its animals that are exposed to the weather. The type and placement will depend on the species, its natural history, captive habits and ability to adapt to abnormal weather conditions. Animals exposed to hot sun will be given access to shade.

Cold/Hot Weather Guidelines

Guidelines for the exhibition or holding of certain species whose health and welfare could be compromised by weather extremes will be developed by Collection Management and will be strictly adhered to. Collection Management can grant exceptions.

Violent Weather Guidelines

Collection Management will develop specific responses to violent weather outside this document. However, these standards will direct that any response to violent weather is predicated on consideration first for the safety of the public and staff and then of the animal.

Transportation of animals

The Zoo recognizes that transporting an animal is an important tool in population management, education, collection development, and veterinary care. These standards emphasize the generally stressful nature of transporting an animal. These standards are directed at reducing, as much as possible, the stress, safety risks and health risks of such transportation.

Collection Management will develop such procedures as are necessary to safely transport animals from institution to institution in as efficient a manner as possible and to ensure that all necessary forms and permits are complete and ready as required and compliance with IATA standards are met.

Generally, animals will not be shipped in weather extremes.

Shipping containers containing animals will be kept out of direct sunlight.

Animals placed in shipping containers that must be held for a time before beginning their journey will be held in the container for no longer than 24 hours before starting their trip.

Animals suspected of being in labor, or that might give birth during transport, will not be transported. Animals caring for neonates generally will not be transported.

Animals being transported in any vehicle for outreach programs, home-rearing or other special uses will be contained in a secure container. Further, the container will be strapped into a seat or tied to the walls or floor whenever possible.

Identification of Animals

These standards establish those methods that are acceptable for marking individual animals.

- Acceptable methods
- tattoo
- transponder chip implant
- ear tag
- ear notch
- leg band
- bracelet
- neck chain and/or pendant
- non toxic, permanent liquid marker

Unacceptable methods

- hot branding
- toe clipping
- scarification

Population management

The Zoo has a role to play in the worldwide efforts to preserve species in the wild and in captivity. It recognizes the importance of managing populations of captive animals on a national, international and local level to help ensure genetic diversity, species vigor and adequate population levels.

The Institution Collection Plan will define breeding strategies and population management plans. This plan will be updated annually to incorporate changes in the collection, facilities and recommendations of conservation programs.

Species Survival Plans

The Zoo supports the concept of Species Survival Plans of the American Zoo and Aquarium Association and will cooperate with any plan to which it is a party to the extent necessary to fulfill the Zoo's mission and objectives as well as those of the SSP's.

Acceptable birth and hatching control methods

The Zoo recognizes the need to control the reproductive potential and/or birth/hatch success of certain species. These standards will set the allowable methods from which staff could select a means, on a case-by-case basis, to exercise such control.

Contraception:

- separation of male and female
- vasectomy/vas deferens plugs
- castration
- antispermatogenesis medication
- hormone alteration
- contraceptive medication
- ovariectomy
- hysterectomy
- contraceptive devices
- antioogenesis medication

Termination of pregnancy:

- chemical abortion, but only if the abortion meets all other care considerations
- surgical abortion, but only if the abortion meets all other care considerations
- euthanasia of aborted fetuses
- abortion under special circumstances

Termination of incubation/egg-laying:

- removal of eggs from nests
- decline to incubate eggs before a notochord is formed
- euthanasia of embryonic eggs
- substitution of artificial eggs for natural eggs under an incubating female
- destroying of nests

Surplus animal disposition

These standards will set the allowable parameters under which animals can be removed from the collection.

The following conditions will be considered when making a decision to remove an animal from the collection:

Need: was the animal needed to enhance genetic diversity, will it decrease group size, how it will affect the Zoo Master Plan, or affect SSP or other cooperative agreements?

Urgency: will the animal be made available for surplus to AZA accredited Zoos or governmental institutions? Is the animal in poor health, or old age?

Resources: Is the Zoo unable to provide appropriate care for this animal or does the Zoo have inadequate facilities?

Documentation: have all avenues been assessed in placing this animal in an appropriate facility, into the wild, private hands, or to be euthanized?

The Zoo will attempt to place animals through AZA accredited Zoological institutions and approved commercial animal dealers.

Animals missing for more than 60 days will be considered lost from the collection and will be removed from the records.

The Zoo will not release, into the wild, any species not native to the targeted ecosystem, unless such release is part of a controlled effort to benefit an endangered species, or part of a controlled effort to reintroduce an extirpated species.

The Zoo will not place any surplus animal at an animal auction, at a game ranch where hunting of the collection is practiced or to any institution or individual where the animal will be used in invasive or terminal research.

The Zoo will not place animals in the private possession of city employees. Animals in possession of current or former employees who received the animal(s) prior to 1 Jan 1996 will be permitted to keep them under agreement.

Accession of animals into the collection

These standards will set the allowable parameters under which animals will be entered into the collection

The following conditions will be considered when making a decision to enter an animal into the collection:

Need: is the animal needed to replace lost stock, enhance genetic diversity, increase group size, address exhibition needs, address the Zoo Master Plan, fulfill SSP or other cooperative agreements?

Urgency: is the animal in urgent need of shelter, veterinary care, or temporary housing pending permanent placement? This may include requests for help from government agencies and/or the AZA/USDI Clearinghouse for confiscated animals.

Resources: does the Zoo have adequate facilities and other resources to provide appropriate care for the animal on either a temporary or long-term basis? How will staffing, budget, and current programs be affected?

Documentation: has adequate documentation been provided regarding the animal's origin, history, lineage, and health? Have all appropriate permits and authorizations been received? If part of a SSP, has the accession been approved by the management committee?

The Zoo will generally try to acquire animals through AZA accredited institutions and registered animal suppliers.

The Zoo will also try to acquire captive-born animals whenever possible to reduce demands on wild stock and promote captive propagation programs and the conservation ethic.

Acquisition of pets and other animals from private individuals will be considered on a case-by-case basis according to the criteria listed above. Additional criteria of public safety (i.e., venomous snake), species rarity and/or value and potential for release or permanent placement can also be considered.

The Zoo will attempt to discourage native and exotic non domestic animals as pets, and can charge a fee, if approved by the governing authority, to accept pets into the collection.

Acceptable breeding strategies

The Zoo recognizes the importance of responsible animal breeding practices for maintaining species integrity, genetic diversity, neonatal health and population viability. These standards will list the allowable strategies that staff can use when manipulating animal reproduction.

In general, breeding strategies will follow those prescribed in Regional Collection Plans, SSP recommendations, husbandry manuals and the Institution Collection Plan. Each species will have on file a management plan that recommends breeding or non-breeding management.

The Zoo will as much as possible try to mate those animals with known lineage, except that "founders," whose lineage might not be known, can be used to increase genetic diversity where appropriate.

Staff will attempt to plan the breeding of each of its species, to ensure that progeny can be cared for properly, to ensure that the Zoo has the resources to care for progeny, to ensure the offspring can be placed in an appropriate facility as needed, and to meet its obligations under SSP.

Acceptable "artificial" strategies:

These standards accept the need to physically or chemically restrain animals, perform surgical procedures or engage in hormone manipulations to accomplish the objectives of "artificial" reproduction. These procedures are allowed only where sufficient technology, methods, and background knowledge are available to the Zoo to support a potentially successful program.

- artificial insemination
- gamete interfallopian transfer
- embryo transplants
- in-vitro fertilization

Acceptable "natural" strategies

These standards accept the likelihood that animals might need to be moved from one institution to another, that valuable breeder animals might have to leave the company of familiar companions to be placed in the company of new companions, and that behavior modification or hormone manipulations might need to be employed to encourage reluctant or incompetent breeders.

- allowing two unrelated animals to breed.
- allowing two different subspecies to breed, only when such combinations are permitted by SSP or by prevailing Zoo industry practices.

Unacceptable breeding strategies:

- cross-breeding two species
- crossing a hybrid with a distinct species or subspecies, unless attempting an "out cross" to recreate phenotype of one of the species, if prescribed by SSP or other plan
- inbreeding deeper than one full generation, unless prescribed by SSP
- crossing two hybrids, unless attempting to recreate the phenotype of one of the species, if   prescribed by SSP or other plan.
- selective breeding for domestication of a wild species
- inbreeding full siblings

Providing nesting/denning sites

The Zoo will provide nesting, denning or birthing site opportunities to any animal as needed to assist parent(s) with birthing/hatching and/or rearing offspring.

Hand-rearing/surrogate rearing of offspring

Collection Management will develop protocol for each situation as it arises.

The Zoo will make every possible effort to encourage and assist parent(s) with rearing their offspring, as long as the safety, health or welfare of offspring or parent(s) are not unduly compromised.

Hand rearing by staff or volunteers will be used in those instances where an offspring cannot be or will not be cared for by its parent(s).

Fostering progeny with another animal of the same or different species will be allowed.

Artificial surrogate parent(s) (such as puppets) can be used, but only as needed to prevent offspring imprinting on humans, and only on offspring that do not need close physical contact with parent(s) or con-specifics to maintain good psychological health. Stuffed toys will be used to provide security "clinging" opportunities to those offspring that exhibit constant clinging behavior early in life.

Staff will attempt, when appropriate, to return offspring to the care of its parent(s), to a foster parent or to the company of its own species as soon as possible, as long as the safety, health or welfare of offspring are not unduly compromised.

Scientific Studies

The Zoo recognizes the value of its collection for increasing the body of knowledge about wild animals, their habits, care, and preservation. The Zoo encourages scientific studies with its collections. Accordingly, these standards will set the parameters under which staff will allow scientific studies to be conducted using the animals.

Collection Management will develop procedures for submission, monitoring and reporting of scientific study projects. Any project involving living animals will be reviewed according to that process before approval can be granted. Further, Collection Management will stop any live animal project that does not meet these standards, has not passed through the review process or does not adhere to Collection Management guidelines. The veterinarian will have authority to stop any project that he or she feels is detrimental to an animal's health or welfare.

The Zoo will not allow any of the following forms of scientific study to be conducted on its collection:

- deprivation of food, water, companionship, veterinary care, sensory stimuli, movement,   parental care or security
- introduction of any pathological condition or application of trauma
- studies involving killing an animal
- studies that introduces painful stimuli to alter behavior or assess reaction
- sensory stimulation beyond that normally encountered by the subject
- application of or introduction of substances onto or into the animal of unknown affect to determine effects

Collection Management will examine and determine on a case-by-case basis the merits of studies that involve phlebotomy, injections, entry into any body orifice or sensory organ, skin or mucosal surface scrapings or any other proposed procedure that can be reasonably expected to stimulate "minor and transient" pain.

The following forms of scientific study are generally acceptable, provided they pass through the review process and adhere to the guidelines developed by Collection Management:

- observations of behavior
- manipulations of nutrient content of food, quantity of food, or palatability of food, provided the objective is not to introduce pathology or deprivation effects
- collection and/or examination of body wastes, secretions or fluids, provided the above pain guidelines are met
- manipulations of an animal's environment to assess changes in behavior or health, provided the objective is not to introduce deprivation effects or pathology

Collection Management will establish guidelines for use of Zoo facilities for studies or teaching, using animals other than those belonging to the Zoo, lending animals out for studies, etc. through its Scientific Studies Program protocol.

Standards of Behavior for Zoo staff

Assurances

A number of local, state and federal agencies impact the Zoo through applications of laws, regulations or procedures. These standards will provide assurance that the Zoo will abide by any such authority.

The Zoological Park will abide by any federal, state or local law or regulation which impacts its operation, will fully cooperate with any and all official inspections, will maintain licensure under the Animal Welfare Act, and will procure and/or maintain the necessary permits to keep, transport or transact business in wildlife.

The Zoological Park will maintain current accredited status with the American Zoo and Aquarium Association and will abide by the code of ethics and regulations of its members.

Ensuring Compliance with the Standards of Care and Exhibition

The Zoo Director will assign such responsibilities and authorities and will exercise such controls as are necessary to ensure compliance with these Standards. Supervisors will develop and implement protocols for the specific care of animals or execution of procedures within the framework of these standards.

Collection Management will develop procedures to fully investigate and respond to complaints and alleged violations of these Standards from any person(s) or organization(s).

It will be the duty of every staff to uphold these standards. Collection Management will develop procedures whereby violation allegations from any Zoo employee or volunteer can be reported to and acted upon at the appropriate levels.

Staff and volunteers will be held to a liberal interpretation of these standards and their intent, rather than a limited interpretation, to protect the welfare of the animals and to provide high quality care.

These standards can be amended under procedures developed by Zoo Director.

Standards are essential for an organization and provide an ethical framework for the organization's work. They are related to the mission and can be extremely detailed or less so depending on again on the organization's mission.

Chapter 16

Measurement Tools

There are a variety of measurement tools that can be used to determine where your organization "is today" for the Strategic Planning process. These tools can also be used to track performance in the Key Result Areas as you work toward the organization's Vision through its Mission.

We'll outline three commonly used measurement tools; surveys (external and internal), flowcharts and activity based costing. In addition, an example of a measurement tool for program areas is also included. This is a special measurement tool that is used if the organization has defined program areas.

Surveys–External

Many businesses and organizations use a simple survey called a customer comment card. These surveys are often voluntary and usually are not filled out by a customer unless something is wrong. This makes the results difficult to interpret. However, a process can be set up that ensures a large and random sample of customers is surveyed by offering a premium for turning in a completed survey card. For example, every 10th customer may be given a card that is rewarded with a free drink when turned in completed at the concession stand.

These types of surveys are often used to gauge what your customers think about your organization. However, they can also be used by staff from other parts of your organization to provide input into how you are meeting Key Result Areas.

Although simple and subject to some error, if done diligently, this type of survey can be very useful in tracking progress in one or more Key Result Areas.

Following is an example of a Customer Comment card distributed to the public:

Customer Comment Card

Week no. _____ Dates

Question*	E	G	A	BA	NA
The facility was clean and the rest rooms were stocked with supplies.					
The grounds and facility were free of litter and well maintained.					
Staff were friendly, knowledgeable, offered their assistance.					
Staff appearance and dress seemed appropriate.					
My experience was at a convenient time and location.					
We provided you a safe experience.					
My experience was what I expected, based on information from the department catalog or other sources.					
Overall Quality of your experience					

*E=Excellent, G=Good, A=Average, BA=Below Average, NA=Not Applicable

These customer comment cards are collected and results entered into a spreadsheet program. Results are tabulated weekly, monthly and annually.

Initial results can be used to establish baseline performance and later to measure progress.

An important consideration is to determine the time period for collecting baseline data. The time period must be long enough for survey results to be fairly consistent. This might involve a month, six months or even a year. However, the longer the time period necessary for collecting baseline data, the longer it takes to measure progress in improving performance.

Weekly reports provide immediate feedback to the staff so that corrections can be made quickly. The effects of those corrections are reflected in subsequent reports. Use of these weekly reports and making timely corrections may enable you to shorten the time period necessary to establish baseline data.

The following is an example of calculated results of customer comments for a week:

Customer Comment Report

Week A   4/27 thru 5/3 Target = 90% each item.

	E	G	A	BA	NA	Ttl	%
The facility was clean	10	23	11	2	1	47	72.28
Free of litter	6	40	12	0	5	63	72.41
Friendly staff	11	30	22	0	6	69	70.63
Appr. staff appear.	2	11	23	0	0	36	60.42
Conv. Time & locat.	14	30	18	2	1	65	71.88
Safe experience	20	22	21	1	0	64	73.83
Expected experience	22	34	14	2	0	72	76.39
Overall quality	34	20	17	3	0	74	78.72

Total Satisfaction Rating   **72.07%**

Surveys–Internal

Internal surveys are used to track compliance with Standards of Care. It is possible to use the same Customer Comment Card for internal surveys but additional ones are also important. Designing these additional surveys for use by all staff members will keep employees familiar with day-to-day standards as well as providing feedback and measures for compliance with care standards.

An example of an internal survey follows which provides measures for quality standards of collection care:

Collection Care Standards
Measures

Date_____Time_____Area_____

By_____

Does the animal have fresh, clean drinking water that is not frozen?

Yes_____   No_____   NA_____

Remarks_____

Is the watering vessel out of public view or not easily identifiable as a watering vessel, or meant to be seen?

Yes_____   No_____   NA_____

Remarks_____

Are watering vessels cleaned and disinfected according to standards?

Yes_____   No_____   NA_____

Remarks_____

Is the watering vessel appropriate for the species that uses it?

Yes_____   No_____   NA_____

Remarks_____

Is the food fed to animals free of mold, spoilage or other deficiencies?

Yes_____   No_____   NA_____

Remarks_____

Are foods stored properly?

Yes_____   No_____   NA_____

Remarks_____

Are food preparation surfaces cleaned and disinfected?

Yes_____   No_____   NA_____

Remarks_____

Is the diet fed to the animal that described by the diet card?

Yes_____   No_____   NA_____

Remarks_____

Is food placed in locations where that species would likely find it in their natural habitat?

Yes_____   No_____   NA_____

Remarks_____

Are food vessels cleaned and disinfected in accordance with the quality standards?

Yes_____   No_____   NA_____

Remarks_____

Is the animal allowed to live in their outside habitats 23 hours per day?

Yes_____   No_____   NA_____

Remarks_____

Has the animal been in holding for no more than 30 days?

Yes_____   No_____   NA_____

Remarks_____

Does indoor habitat lighting meet the standards of spectrum and light cycles?

Yes_____   No_____   NA_____

Remarks_____

Does the indoor habitat have posted the range of acceptable levels of light, lighting cycles (if natural sunlight is not available), humidity and temperature for the animals living in them?

Yes_____   No_____   NA_____

Remarks_____

Are doors closed and unused lights turned out in service areas so they are not visible to the public?

Yes_____   No_____   NA_____

Remarks_____

Does the habitat present an acceptable representation of the animal's natural habitat?

Yes_____   No_____   NA_____

Remarks_____

Is the habitat free from hazards that might result in injury or death to the animal?

Yes_____   No_____   NA_____

Remarks_____

Is the habitat clean?

Yes_____   No_____   NA_____

Remarks_____

Are tools and equipment used in cleaning procedure clean?

Yes_____   No_____   NA_____

Remarks_____

Are drains and drain baskets clean?

Yes_____   No_____   NA_____

Remarks_____

Is standing water and/or mud in the habitat minimized?

Yes_____   No_____   NA_____

Remarks_____

Is animal bedding clean and free of hazards such as wire and debris?

Yes_____   No_____   NA_____

Remarks_____

Is the animal habitat temperature within the posted ranges?

Yes_____   No_____   NA_____

Remarks_____

Is the habitat free of pests?

Yes_____   No_____   NA_____

Remarks_____

Is the service area clean and neat, free of refuse or debris?

Yes_____   No_____   NA_____

Remarks_____

Is the habitat and service area secured?

Yes_____   No_____   NA_____

Remarks_____

Are service doors or gates closed?

Yes_____   No_____   NA_____

Remarks_____

Is the animal identified by a label or graphic?

Yes_____   No_____   NA_____

Remarks_____

Does the animal have shelter from sun, wind, rain, snow, etc.?

Yes_____   No_____   NA_____

Remarks_____

Does the animal have identification?

Yes_____   No_____   NA_____

Remarks_____

Results are tallied and recorded in a spreadsheet. One can not only tally the results of the surveys, but also the person that did the surveys and how many were done. This can provide additional information for staff performance evaluations. A simple example follows:

Month	yes	no	%	Target
Jan	187	55	77	90
Feb	341	127	73	90
Mar	670	222	75	90
Apr	804	216	79	90
May	536	128	81	90
Jun	617	190	76	90
Jul	278	61	82	90
Aug	754	121	86	90
Sep	879	213	80	90

Oct	456	165	73	90
Nov	233	88	73	90
Dec	123	43	74	90

Flowcharts

Processes can be defined by using graphical representations of each step and presented in a flowchart. By using graphical representations, a variety of steps and their functions in the process can be easily presented. The flowchart indicates points at which decisions must be made and by whom and what happens in the process when a particular decision is made.

Standard flowcharting symbols are used to indicate steps in the process. These symbols represent steps such as start or end point, action, flow direction, decision, etc.

The following flowchart is a simple one detailing the process of depositing fees for services. It compares two different approaches to the process on the same flowchart. There is only one decision point that is necessary. Flowcharts can be very complicated with many decision points and alternate paths. By representing these decision points and the path decisions take one can evaluate the efficiency of the process and make changes that can streamline the process. Often one flowchart is used to document a current process while a different one is used to document an improved process. The point of changing the process is to maintain the effectiveness of the process but increase its efficiency.

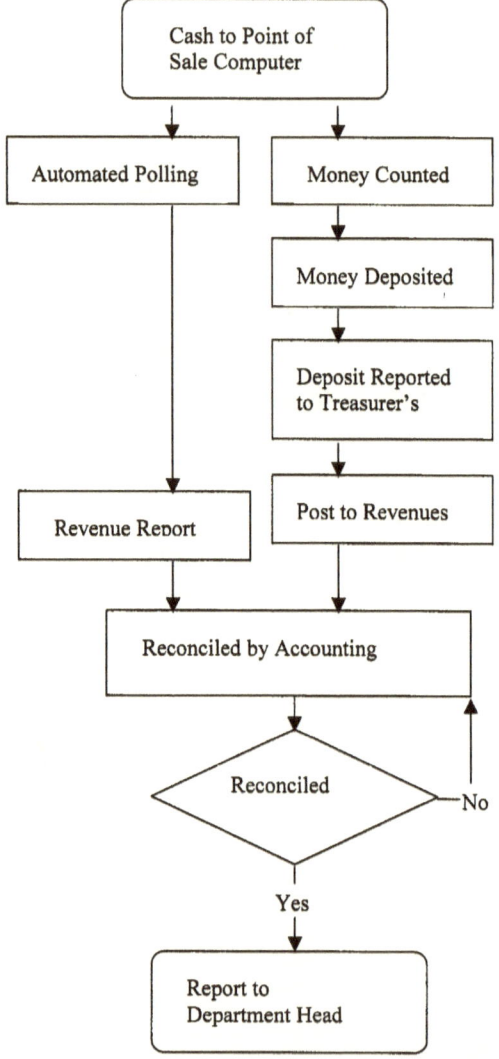

Activity Based Costing

Core Activities consume resources. In fact, the three core activities discussed elsewhere will consume 100% of an organization's resources. Activity Based Costing (ABC) is a tool that defines the cost of a given activity.

Every activity has direct costs and indirect costs. Direct costs are usually easy to define. For example, the costs of utilities and maintenance contracts can easily be assigned to the core activity of Facility Care. There may be instances where a direct cost is applied to two or more core activities. Servicing public rest rooms is an example. Repairing a public rest room is a Facility Care activity while cleaning those rest rooms is a Customer Care activity. Often the same staff is used. In this case the Maintenance Supervisor must estimate or track the time staff takes to repair the rest rooms and the time staff takes to clean the rest rooms.

An organization that is part of a parent organization may not directly pay for some services such as marketing. Yet marketing is a real cost in the Customer Care activity. One way to determine this marketing cost is to ask the marketing staff to estimate or assign a cost to your organization. Another method is to determine what percentage your organization's total budget is of the whole organization and use that percentage to determine the marketing cost. This same process can be used for many costs that are not wholly found in your organization's budget.

Indirect costs are more difficult to define and some estimation may be necessary to make the costing reports work. For example, administrative costs are indirect. Some administrative time is spent supporting each core activity. An estimate can be made of the cost of administrative support for each activity and used in the ABC report.

In some organizations in which a substantial amount of resources are provided by the parent organization, the ABC report should indicate that the true cost of activity exceeds the organization's budget but is within the parent organization's budget. One of the reasons for doing an ABC report is to determine true costs of the core activities.

Activity Based Costing uses four elements to determine costs:

- Cost pools–budget categories and item details
- Quantity–amount of time or money or product consumed
- Drivers–unit cost of the cost pool (e.g. $12.50 per hour)
- Outputs–result of the quantity times the driver

For each core activity it is necessary to define cost pools, determine quantities and assign drivers. The resulting ABC report will reflect the true costs of the core activity with both direct and indirect costs. That information can be used for additional analysis.

The ABC report is best tracked using a spreadsheet application. Once set up it is only necessary to input the quantities for a given time period and adjust drivers if needed. These reports are best done monthly and consolidated for an annual report. The first reports provide a baseline or "where you are today." Subsequent reports provide performance tracking.

An example of an ABC spreadsheet for Customer Care follows:

Activity Based
Costing

Activity – Customer Care		Jan		Year

Direct costs

Cost pools		Quantity	Drivers	Outputs
Personnel				
	Admission clerk	146.25 hrs	$10.92 hr rate+benefits	$1,596.48
	Admission clerk	0 hrs	$12.66 hr rate+benefits	$0.00
	Temps validators	226.75 hrs	$5.72 hr rate+benefits	$1,297.01
	Temps maint	0 hrs	$5.50 hr rate+benefits	$0.00
			Total	$2,893.49
Contractual				
	Printing tickets	1,648 ea	$0.01 ea	$16.48
	Printing maps	300 ea	$0.02 ea	$6.00
	Advertising	ea	$2,300.00 yr	$0.00
			Total	$22.48
Commodities				
	Glass cleaner	1 gal	$1.88	$1.88
	Sponges	4 ea	$0.59	$2.36
	Deodorant block	18 ea	$0.33	$5.94
	Deodorant screens	4 ea	$0.96	$3.84
	Toilet tissue	60 ea	$0.32	$19.20
	Trash bags	200 ea	$0.12	$24.00
	Hand soap	2 ea	$2.82	$5.64
	All purpose cleaner	0.5 gal	$3.06	$1.53
	Bleach	0.25 gal	$1.10	$0.28
	Air spray	2 ea	$5.83	$11.66
	Bowl brush	0.5 ea	$1.73	$0.87
	Mop heads	1 ea	$3.28	$3.28
	Hygiene pads	4 ea	$0.13	$0.52
	Office supplies	0.083 annual	$300.00 yr	$24.90
			Total	$105.89
Sales tax				
	sales tax	$5,709.23 rev	6.15%	$330.77

Capital Outlay

Total Direct Cost				$3,352.63
				68.81%

Indirect Costs				
Cost Pools		Quantity	Drivers	Outputs
Personnel				
	Administration	31.1 hrs/mo	$15.94 hr rate+benefits	$830.84
	Maintenance	62 hrs/mo	$11.12 hr rate+benefits	$689.13
			Total	$1,519.97
Contractural				
Commodities				
Capital Outlay				
Total Indirect Costs				$1,519.97
				31.19%
Total Costs				$4,872.61
	Number of visitors			5,338
	Cost per visitor			$0.91
	Revenue per visitor			$1.07
	Ratio of cost to revenue			85.35%

Notice that not only is the core activity cost determined but also cost per visitor and revenue per visitor is figured. This additional information can be quite useful. The example shows only one month of activity. Each month should be calculated in a spreadsheet and the monthly figures combined into a year-end report.

Program Measurements

The following example is a spreadsheet that is used to collect data and to provide a number of calculations that can determine the status of programs. This example is comprehensive in that it calculates the status of all the programs of an organization in a given month. Each month is recorded and calculated. At the end of the year all monthly figures are added together to provide a year-end report of all program areas. Baseline numbers are determined based on the previous year's performance or by annual planning of the staff usually based on the approved budget for the current year or both.

The data area of the spreadsheet indicates the staff member responsible for collecting the data each month. The report area of the spreadsheet reports only effectiveness and efficiency measures. Effectiveness measures "are you doing the right thing." Efficiency measures "are you doing the right thing well."

Program Measures

Data

	Baseline	Aug
General Curator		
Quality standards animal care	90.00%	75%
Number of specimens	375	371
Expenses/month col manag	$54,431	$47,447
# cons managed specimens	187.5	175
# *in situ* programs	5	5
Expenses/month cons/sci	$533	$35
Office Supervisor		
Best of Community	2	2
Event attendance		3044
Number of events	6	6
Cost of event		$80
Customer satisfaction	90%	77%
Admission target	$393,865	$60,813.28
Admission actual	$393,865	$49,244.00
Attendance	225011	26966
Director		
Visitor care cost	$0.51	$0.42
Fund raising goal for year	$500,000	$500,000
Capital funds raised to date	$500,000	$100,000
public funds raised to date	$200,000	$0
private funds raised to date	$300,000	$100,000
Community residents	125000	125000
Accredited by AZA	yes	yes
Licensed by USDA	yes	yes
Education Director		
# class offerings	10	10
# classes filled	10	8
classes income	$7,500.00	$2,686.00
classes expense	$3,500.00	$740.49
Operation Supervisor		
Quality standards facility care		
Cost of facility care/mo	$36,270	$33,869.20
# exhibits	51	51
# exhibits w/labels	51	45

Program Measures

Report Collection Management	Measure	Target	Actual
Effectiveness Measure	% compliance with Quality Standards for Animal Care	90.00%	75.00%
Efficiency Measure	Cost of care per specimen/mon	$145.15	$127.89

Community	Measure	Target	Actual
Effectiveness Measure	Recognitions in "Best of Community" program	2	2
	Number of special events	6	6
Efficiency Measure	Cost of event per visitor	$0.00	$0.00

Conservation/Science	Measure	Target	Actual
Effectiveness Measure	% of conservation managed species	50.00%	47.17%
	number of *in situ* programs	5	5
Efficiency Measure	Cost of programs per species/ month	$2.84	$0.20

Customer Service	Measure	Target	Actual
Effectiveness Measure	% customer satisfaction	90.00%	76.78%
Efficiency Measure	Cost of visitor care per visitor	$0.51	$0.42

Development	Measure	Target	Actual
Effectiveness Measure	% of fund raising goals met public & private	100.00%	20.00%
Efficiency Measure	Ratio of private to public funds raised	150.00%	NA

Program Measures

Education	Measure	Target	Actual
Effectiveness Measure	% of class offerings filled	100.00%	80.00%
	% of exhibits with labels	100.00%	88.24%
Efficiency Measure	Ratio of income to expense for class offerings	214.29%	362.73%

Facility Management	Measure	Target	Actual
Effectiveness Measure	% compliance with Quality Standards for Facility Care	0.00%	0.00%
Efficiency Measure	Cost of facility care per city resident/month	$0.29	$0.27

Marketing	Measure	Target	Actual
Effectiveness Measure	% of admission revenue target met	100.00%	80.98%
Efficiency Measure	Per capita admission income	$1.75	$1.83

Administration	Measure	Target	Actual
Effectiveness Measure	Accredited by AZA	yes	yes
	Licensed by USDA	yes	yes

These are just a few tools that can be used to measure various aspects of your organization's key result areas and programs. There are many others including bar charts, cause and effect diagrams, control charts, histograms, etc. A good manager will learn how to use the various measurement tools and apply them to provide the most effective means to report performance measures.

Chapter 17

Fund Raising

Most unmanageable organizations need to raise funds, often for capital improvements but also for operating expenses. It is by far easier to raise capital funds than operating expenses. A lot of organizations make the mistake of raising capital funds but fail to plan for increased operating expenses and quickly get into financial trouble. The way your organization raises funds for both capital improvements and operating revenue depends on the type of governing authority that is in place and the legal and policy restrictions that the governing authority has.

There are two main purposes for an organization's fund raising activities: to raise money for a project or operation and to involve the community in the organization's vision and mission.

Unmanageable organizations often exist to improve the quality of life for a community but are usually not part of basic or core services of a community such as fire or police protection. Government funding, therefore, is often inadequate and tax money for improvement projects is not always popular. Fund raising from private sources or grants becomes important for the organization to improve and/or expand the physical plant. Organizations without a physical plant don't have this fund raising task to deal with.

Fundraising for capital improvements is difficult but not impossible. The real key is knowing your community and being aware of what else is going in the community as well as how the community accepts your organization's vision and mission. There are many organizations in a community that may be fund raising at one time or another. Every community has a capacity for giving. Knowing what other organizations are fund raising and being aware of the fund raising capacity will help in determining fund raising timing and monetary goals that can be met.

It is also important to know which giving organizations to target for fundraising. Certain businesses may have a long relationship with your organization and would be interested in supporting your organization with capital gifts. Other businesses may wish to align themselves with your organization because of your organization's popularity in the community or your organization's commitment to a similar vision or mission. If you can identify giving organizations and businesses that are a good fit for your fund raising campaign it is a good idea to keep them informed of your organization's future plans and the progress of current projects. You might consider a special newsletter that keeps current and prospective donors up to date on your organization's capital projects and plans.

Many organizations hire a fund raising company that will assist the organization in organizing and carrying out a fund raising campaign. The fund raising company can identify potential donors, determine the level of commitment those donors may make and establish procedures by which those donations can be secured. Some fundraisers are better than others and most are expensive. Select the fund raising company carefully. The success of the campaign can depend on the quality of the fundraiser. You might find a local company that is well known and respected in your community that will be accepted better by donors than a company that comes from another community and doesn't really know the donors or the community. A local company would be the best choice but may not always be possible.

Donors like to have recognition for their contributions. This includes donors at all levels. One of the challenges for an organization is to determine what types of recognition are possible for the campaign and what levels of donations will result in the type of recognition. If you are raising money for a building, it is not unusual for the building to be named after a major donor. Your first challenge is to determine if naming a building after a major donor is appropriate for your organization. If so, then the level of the donation that qualifies for naming must be determined. I believe the bar should be set high for this acknowledgement. I have seen a donor's name given to a project in which the donor provided only 10% of the project cost. I think the bar should be set for at least 80% of the cost of the project for the entire project to receive a donor's name.

However, a project can be divided up into many smaller donor opportunities. For example, if a building project has a number of rooms, each room can be named for a donor that gives a certain amount to the total project. I've seen chairs in an auditorium with names of donors on the back. Bricks are often sold for a sidewalk or patio with donors names inscribed in them. Benches can be sold with nameplates on them. Recognition plaques in gardens, in front of exhibits, on about anything can be used to recognize donors. Your fundraising campaign will benefit from determining all the possibilities and ensuring your potential donors have a variety of giving opportunities.

It is also important to recognize donors in some sort of public way with an organized event. It may be a preview to the project prior to a public opening or a special event like a gala that recognizes your donors. Keeping these donors involved with your organization will help with a future fundraising campaign.

Another way to keep major donors interested in your project is to ask for the donor to have a representative attend planning sessions for the project. This involves the donor and the input from the representative can be very valuable. It provides a different perspective that you may not have considered that will make the project better.

Fundraising for operating expenses is a very different process and is far more difficult. For the donor, there is often little to show for the donation, certainly nothing that is permanent such as a building or even a brick.

However, there are some ways that raising funds for operating expenses can be accomplished. It is also possible to create partnerships that will provide services that can reduce the need for funds.

An interesting way to provide operating revenue is to build an operating endowment into a capital project. If the capital project is $1 million, then fundraise for $1.25 million and put the balance in an endowment for operations or maintenance of the project. These numbers will vary depending on the type of project and the anticipated operating and/or maintenance costs. Certainly, some projects cost more to maintain than others.

Some donors will agree to sponsor an exhibit or special project for a period of time with appropriate recognition. An exhibit that has already been constructed, for example, may interest a donor for sponsorship. It is understood that the donation of funds will be used for operation and maintenance of the exhibit. The agreement should be in a contractual form so that all parties know what is expected. The agreement may provide for the donor's employees to provide a workday for the exhibit or at the facility in addition to the cash donation. This type of arrangement can work for a special project such as an outreach program. The important part of these arrangements is that the donor is appropriately recognized and the organization receives adequate support. In some organizations, these arrangements are very long term and expand to include additional projects as the relationship becomes more beneficial to both parties.

A few organizations have successfully raised operating funds by soliciting direct public donations. There are a variety of ways to do this. There are telethons, telemarketing, direct mail, donation boxes, bake sales, etc. Some of these ways are more successful than others. Some organizations may solicit an annual donation but allow the donation to be billed or withdrawn from the donor's account monthly. Sometimes premiums are offered but it is important for the donor to elect not to receive the premium. Donors do like to be recognized but often prefer a special tour, a special recognition function or even to be asked to volunteer with the organization.

One of the most successful fundraising campaigns at the Topeka Zoo was called Noah's Ark. Several local businesses agreed to give the Zoo a certain amount of money for each product wrapper that was turned in. The public was invited to turn in product wrappers at certain locations. The money raised was pledged to purchase certain animals for the Zoo. Whenever an animal was purchased there was a recognition plaque that indicated the animal was provided to the Zoo by the Noah's Ark campaign. There was a great deal of public participation because it was easy to do and there was recognition although not individual. All who donated wrappers felt a part of the campaign and were proud of their part in obtaining animals for the Zoo. Collecting product wrappers was simple and many of the community's children became involved with their families and school classes in collecting activities. Many of those children, now adults, remember those activities fondly and continued their interest in the Zoo.

Another type of operating support donation is the donation of in-kind services. It may be easier for a donor business to provide a service for your organization than to donate cash. For example, you might find a printing company willing to donate all your organization's printing needs or an airline to provide for the travel needs of your organization's staff. In all cases, it is important to have a written agreement that will establish the parameters of the donation. Most donors will not feel comfortable with an open-ended donation and you should be ready to suggest the acceptable limits of the donation. You must also establish appropriate recognition of the donor for the services provided. Some organizations trade services. If your organization is a fee based public facility you might trade a certain number of admissions for the donation of services or possibly free tickets to a special event or even inclusion for an exhibit preview.

In all fundraising, whether for capital projects or operating expenses, there are several common conditions:

- Ensure your fundraising is consistent with your organization's vision and mission.
- Use professionals, either your own staff or an outside firm to do the fundraising.
- Don't sell your organization short by accepting donations to meet short-term needs that don't meet long-term goals.
- Be sure your fundraising activities meet the legal and ethical restraints of the law and your governing authority.
- Adequately recognize your donors.

Government governing authority can very much restrict your ability to fundraise for your organization. In many governments, donations must go to the general fund and cannot be accepted by the organization itself. Some government governing authorities may not allow donations at all. For this reason, organizations with a government governing authority often must have a private organization that can receive and disperse donations to the organization. One way this can be done is to create a Foundation whose charter is to raise funds and support the organization. The government governing authority must often approve this arrangement. Having a legal contract defining this arrangement is best.

In addition, it is best to have a contract between the government governing authority and the fundraising support organization for each individual project. This is especially important for projects in which both parties provide funds and/or services to the project. For example, the fundraising support organization may provide the cash but the government governing authority provides the engineering services, legal services, etc. Generally, an organization that has a government governing authority legally owns the organization's facilities. Contracts ensure that the ownership transfer, at the time construction is complete, is clearly defined.

Some managers feel they can adequately do fundraising without outside help. Not true. As a manager, your role should be to know what is necessary to pull together all the fundraising, support groups and the governing authority so that successful fundraising can be facilitated.

It is also a fact that the majority of fundraising is done between highly influential friends in the community. They help each other out with pet projects they have adopted as important to them or their business or the community.

For most projects, it is important for the community to become involved. Often, announcing the fundraising drive and soliciting donations from the community accomplish this. However, this public announcement should be withheld until a large portion of the needed funds has already been pledged. Some organizations do not announce the fundraising drive until 60% of the needed funds have been pledged. Other organizations will wait for a larger percentage to be pledged before announcing. The funds raised by community solicitations are difficult to raise in substantial amounts because the donations are usually small. These donations are best considered as a way to involve the community in the project rather than a major source of funds for the project.

Successful fundraising can be a great way to enhance an organization's physical plant, provide new exhibits, provide new or expanded programs and assist with operating expenses. Successful fundraising can also be a great way for the organization to publicize its vision and mission and involve the community in the organization.

Chapter 18

Budgeting

If your new job starts after the operating budget has been approved, spend as much time as possible understanding what has been established. If your new job starts just before a new budget is being written, you need to quickly apply some budgeting techniques that will get a good first budget adopted.

There are few unmanageable organizations that don't need money. Budgeting for needed funds is often a struggle and the budgeting process in these organizations is usually illogical and harmful to the organization.

Ideally, the best budgeting process is zero-based budgeting. You start with a clean slate; no money budgeted. You then build the budget by determining annual needs for each area of the budget. The best way to do this is to base needs on the results from Activity Based Costing.

Previously, examples of using Activity Based Costing for determining expenditures of Core Activities were presented. Activity Based Costing can also be used to track expenditures in Programs. In fact, setting up a spreadsheet or database in which Program expenses are tracked that feed into the expenses of the Core Activity will provide valuable information for zero-based budgeting. For example, the core activity of Collection Care might be made up of programs such as; conservation, veterinary care and care of the collections.

Activity Based Costing can provide the basis for a budget request by showing, at multiple levels, needed funding. In addition, new programs or adjustments to current programs can also be well documented by estimating new program costs that feed into Core Activities. New programs and/or program adjustments must be well documented in the budget request. Experience with Activity Based Costing can assist in providing accurate estimates of new funding needs.

A program summary sheet follows:

PROPOSED OPERATING BUDGET

Department: Completed By:
Division: Date: 16 Apr
Section/Subdivision: Reviewed By:

Program: Conservation/Science

BUDGET COMMENTS / EXPLANATIONS
(NON-PERSONNEL)

Program Resources

Tax Subsidy	Earned Rev	Donations	Total
$0	$5,625	$6,200	$11,825

This summary sheet is only one of several that show a budget in a program format. This particular one provides information on where resources to fund the program are derived. You can use a line item budget to produce these summary sheets or use the results of Activity Based Costing reports.

Unfortunately, most unmanageable organizations do not have an ideal budgeting environment. You may be required to use zero-based budgeting but budget approval actually is based on arbitrary numbers, which are often amounts expended in the previous year. This is a political answer to budgeting and is very unenlightened. It is a short-term way to budget rather than dealing with long term funding needs. It is not surprising that government governing authorities have the worst track record in budgeting.

The budgeting process for organizations with a government governing authority often involves the submission of the amounts spent in the previous year, the amount estimated to be spent in the current year and the amount requested for the budget year. All these figures are on a line item basis. For example, utility expenses are a line item. There is no relationship to a Program or Core Activity except that utility costs may be part of one or more Programs and/or Core Activities.

Let's say the utility costs for the previous year were $50,000 but the winter and summer were mild. Estimated utility costs for the current year are $100,000 and the requested amount for the budget to be approved is $110,000. The increase is due to inflation. You know that normal utility costs are $100,000 per year based on Activity Based Costing reports of the last 5 years. Guess which number the government governing authority will use to approve the utility cost request. $50,000. Politicians will always pick the lowest number without consideration of mitigating circumstances. There is also never a provision for utility costs that may exceed the normal year's need due to weather extremes. This same process occurs for each line item. While politicians claim they are only interested in the bottom line, you won't find one that doesn't scrutinize detailed expenses.

So, what is wrong with someone scrutinizing the details of a budget? Nothing, as long as the budget is looked at historically at the Program and Core Activity level with Activity Based Costing reports. Everything, if the previous expenditures by line item are the only data considered. As a manager, you need to provide the Activity Based Costing reports.

You receive $50,000 for utilities and you spent $100,000. You don't get additional funding for the normal utility costs and must cut other areas of the budget to make up the difference because you cannot exceed the spending limit of the bottom line. Those cuts then become permanent in subsequent years. The result of this budgeting process is a continually decreasing budget. This process is another aspect of why unmanageable organizations are so unmanageable.

Following is an example of a line item budget in a process described above:

		1999	2000	2000	2001
		Actual $	Adopted $	Estimate $	Request $
	Personnel				
1001	Regular Employees - FT	287,786	297,892	287,466	306,829
1002	Regular Employees - PT	9,694	9,844	9,499	10,139
1004	Temporary Employees	3,146	0	0	0
1005	Overtime Pay	215	0	0	0
1006	Holiday Pay	217	0	0	0
1008	Shift Differential	0	0	0	0
1010	Sick Leave	0	0	0	0
1012	Vacation Leave	0	0	0	0
1014	Training	0	0	0	0
1016	Jury Duty Pay	0	0	0	0
1017	Military Leave	0	0	0	0
1018	Funeral Leave	0	0	0	0
1020	Out-of Classification Pay	0	0	0	0
1024	Comp Time	240	2,000	1,930	2,060
1025	Bonus Pay	0	0	0	0
1026	Administrative Leave	0	0	0	0
1050	Accrued Vacation Time	0	0	0	0
1055	Provisions for Salary Adjustme	0	0	0	0
1057	Salary Market Adjustment	0	0	0	0
1201	Social Security	22,391	23,104	22,295	23,797
1202	KPERS	8,759	9,909	9,562	10,206
1204	Health Insurance	20,099	22,016	21,245	22,676
1206	Unemployment Tax	0	0	0	0
1270	Retirement Reserve Contributi	1,439	3,078	2,970	3,170
1280	Workman's Comp	2,540	2,732	2,636	2,814
1297	Payroll Contra, W&S Reimburs	0	0	0	0
	Total Personnel	356,526	370,575	357,605	381,692
	Contractual				
2001	Electricity	0	0	0	
2002	Natural Gas	0	0	0	
2003	Water	0	0	0	
2004	Solid Waste Disposal	0	0	0	
2005	Sewer Service	0	0	0	
2008	Storm Water	0	0	0	
2101	Postage	4,405	850	820	850
2102	Telephone	1,783	1,800	1,737	1,800
2103	Fax	0	0	0	
2104	Data Acquisition	0	0	0	
2105	Two Way Radio Voice	0	100	97	100
2200	Individual and Contract Service	0	0	0	
2201	Temp Employee from Agency	0	0	0	

		1999 Actual $	2000 Adopted $	2000 Estimate $	2001 Request $
2202	Instructors	0	0	0	
2203	Athletic Officials	0	0	0	
2204	Performing Artists	0	0	0	
2205	Accounting	0	0	0	
2206	Data Processing	10	25,209	24,327	25,209
2208	Education/Training	0	300	290	300
2209	Architectural	0	0	0	
2210	Tennis Pro	0	0	0	
2213	Tennis Pro	0	0	0	
2215	Engineering/City	0	0	0	
2225	Engineering/Consultant	0	0	0	
2226	Medical	0	0	0	
2240	Administrative Fees	0	0	0	
2245	Organizational Dues	2,205	2,000	1,930	1,500
2246	Subscriptions Periodicals	147	350	338	150
2297	Security Services	0	0	0	
2299	Other/Individual and Prof Cont	209	1,000	965	1,000
2300	Education/Travel	0	0	0	
2301	In Town Mileage	515	600	579	600
2302	Out of Town Travel	0	250	241	250
2305	Public Transportation	0	0	0	
2310	Registration/Tuition	664	900	869	900
2312	Meals/Lodging	250	0	0	
2315	Advisory Board Meals	8	0	0	
2400	Printing and Advertising	19	0	0	
2401	Printing - Forms, Etc.	523	2,000	1,930	700
2402	Printing - Reports	228	500	483	500
2412	Advertising	24,699	29,760	28,718	33,250
2415	Photo Copies	429	500	483	500
2499	Other Printing and Advertising	0	0	0	
2500	Insurance	0	0	0	
2501	Worker's Compensation	0	0	0	
2502	Vehicle Liability	0	0	0	
2503	Vehicle Casualty	0	0	0	
2506	General Liability	0	0	0	
2507	General Casualty	0	0	0	
2509	Liability/Dishonesty and Crime	332	0	0	
2511	Surety and Fidelity Bonds	0	0	0	
2512	Comprehensive Business Offic	0	0	0	
2513	Comprehensive Data Process	0	0	0	
2514	Inland Marine Floater	0	0	0	
2516	Boilers	0	0	0	
2599	Other Insurance	0	400	386	200
2600	Maintenance Buildings and Gr	0	0	0	

		1999	2000	2000	2001
		Actual $	Adopted $	Estimate $	Request $
2601	Grounds and Improvements	0	0	0	
2602	Buildings/Exterior Structural	0	0	0	
2603	Buildings/Auxiliary Equipment	0	0	0	
2604	Building Interior Remodel/Red	0	0	0	
2610	Emergency Repair	0	0	0	
2700	Maintenance Machinery and E	0	0	0	
2701	Motor Vehicles	0	0	0	
2702	Fleet Maintenance Charges	0	0	0	
2710	Office Equipment	0	3,200	3,088	500
2720	Communication Equipment	0	0	0	
2730	Safety Equipment	0	0	0	
2740	Construction Equipment	0	0	0	
2750	Facilities Equipment	0	0	0	
2760	Computer Equipment	0	0	0	
2799	Other Maintenance, Machinery	0	0	0	
2800	Rent	0	0	0	
2801	Data Processing Equipment	0	0	0	
2802	Office Equipment and Other	284	100	97	100
2803	Maintenance Equipment	0	0	0	
2804	Portable Restrooms	0	0	0	
2805	Maintenance Equipment	0	0	0	
2810	Vehicles	0	0	0	
2820	Office Space	13,660	13,660	13,182	13,660
2821	Facilities	0	0	0	
2825	Rent/Storage Space	0	0	0	
2830	Uniforms/Clothing	0	0	0	
2899	Rent/Other	0	0	0	
2900	Other Purchased Services	10	0	0	
2903	Court Costs/Filing Fees	0	0	0	
2904	Recording Fees	105	0	0	
2905	Software Licenses	0	300	290	100
2906	Other License Fees	0	130	125	50
2910	Background Checks	5	0	0	
2923	Recertification	0	0	0	
2926	Purchased - Building Security.	0	0	0	
2935	Inspections	0	0	0	
2942	Janitorial Services	0	0	0	
2945	Care of Property	0	25	24	25
2948	Garment Cleaning	0	0	0	
2955	Public Information System	0	250	241	250
2960	Moving Expenses	0	0	0	
2999	Purchased Services/Other	0	0	0	
	Total Contractural	50,490	84,184	81,238	82,494

		1999 Actual $	2000 Adopted $	2000 Estimate $	2001 Request $
	Taxes				
3201	Sales Taxes	0	0	0	
3204	Damages and Claims - Gen Li	0	0	0	
3207	Payment in Lieu of Taxes	0	0	0	
3220	Taxes (Property)	0	0	0	
3299	Other Payments	0	50	48	50
	Total Tax	0	50	48	50
	Commodities				
4000	Office Supplies	300	0	0	300
4001	Paper, Letterhead, Forms	264	650	627	650
4002	Photo Copy Supplies	1	360	347	360
4003	Filing and Storage Supplies	213	150	145	150
4004	Typing and Writing Supplies	213	300	290	300
4005	Calculator Supplies	0	0	0	
4007	Computer Supplies	42	850	820	300
4010	Office Equipment	315	200	193	300
4011	Telephone Supplies	0	0	0	
4099	Office Supplies/Other	0	0	0	
4100	Consumable Tools	28	0	0	
4101	Hand Tools	0	0	0	
4110	Keys (blank and new ones)	0	0	0	
4199	Other Consumable Tools	0	25	24	25
4200	Agriculture Supplies	0	0	0	
4201	Seed	0	0	0	
4202	Fertilizer	0	0	0	
4203	Insecticide and/or Herbicide	0	0	0	
4204	Plants	0	0	0	
4205	Soils and Potting Materials	0	0	0	
4209	Landscaping Materials	0	0	0	
4299	Agriculture Supplies/Other	0	0	0	
4300	Drug and Lab Supplies	0	0	0	
4301	Laboratory Chemicals	0	0	0	
4302	Drug Supplies	0	0	0	
4310	Medical Supplies	0	0	0	
4320	Laboratory Equipment	0	0	0	
4399	Other	0	0	0	
4400	Food	0	0	0	
4401	Food/Meeting Expense	372	500	483	450
4405	Food Service Supplies	32	0	0	
4410	Food for Animals	0	0	0	
4500	Materials for Street Maintenan	0	0	0	

		1999	2000	2000	2001
		Actual $	Adopted $	Estimate $	Request $
4501	Asphalt	0	0	0	
4502	Rock/Chat/Sand	0	0	0	
4504	De-Icing Chemicals	0	0	0	
4510	Concrete	0	0	0	
4520	Signs and Markers	0	0	0	
4600	Clothing	0	0	0	
4601	Uniforms	0	0	0	
4602	Safety Shoes, etc.	0	0	0	
4603	Hard Hats, etc.	0	0	0	
4605	Protective Clothing	0	0	0	
4699	Clothing/Other	0	0	0	
4701	Propane and/or Butane	0	0	0	
4702	Fuel Oil and/or Kerosene	0	0	0	
4703	Acetylene and/or Oxygen	0	0	0	
4710	Lubricants	0	0	0	
4799	Fuel and Lubricants Other	0	0	0	
4801	Buildings	0	0	0	
4810	Repair Parts - Equipment	0	100	97	
4830	Grounds	0	0	0	
4840	Office Machines	0	0	0	
4850	Safe Equipment	0	0	0	
4870	Chemical Feed	0	0	0	
4899	Other Repair Parts, Non Motor	0	0	0	
4900	Building Maintenance Supplies	0	0	0	
4901	Light Bulbs and Other Electrica	0	0	0	
4902	Cleaning Supplies	0	25	24	25
4903	Preservatives, Wax, etc.	0	0	0	
4904	Paper Products	0	0	0	
4905	Lumber and Hardware	0	0	0	
4910	Paint	0	0	0	
4915	Filters	0	0	0	
4920	Plumbing	0	0	0	
4925	Heating and Ventilation and Ai	0	0	0	
4930	Electrical Parts	0	0	0	
4999	Building Maintenance Supply/(	0	0	0	
5001	Fuel	0	0	0	
5002	Lubricants	0	0	0	
5003	Tires	0	0	0	
5004	Repair Parts	0	0	0	
5099	Motor Vehicle Supply/Other	0	0	0	
5200	Recreation Supplies	0	0	0	
5210	Sports Equipment	0	0	0	
5220	Trophies	0	0	0	
5230	Art Supplies	0	0	0	

		1999 Actual $	2000 Adopted $	2000 Estimate $	2001 Request $
5240	Craft Supplies	0	0	0	
5299	Recreation Supply/Other	60	200	193	100
5300	Photo Supplies	0	0	0	
5301	Photo/Film	30	50	48	50
5302	Photo Processing Supplies	178	100	97	200
5303	Batteries	0	0	0	
5399	Photo Supplies/Other	0	0	0	
5400	Merchandise for Resale	0	0	0	
5410	Food	0	0	0	
5420	Souvenirs and Novelties	378	50	48	125
5430	Recreation Supplies	0	0	0	
5499	Other	0	0	0	
5500	Books and Reference Material	21	150	145	75
5501	Books	97	200	193	100
5502	Reference Materials	0	100	97	25
5600	Other Materials and Supplies	0	0	0	
	Total Commodities	2,544	4,010	3,870	3,535
	Capital Outlay				
7006	Buildings	0	0	0	
7008	Improvement to Land/Other	0	0	0	
7010	Motor Vehicles	0	0	0	
7012	Maintenance Equipment	0	0	0	
7022	Furniture	0	0	0	
7024	Office Equipment	0	0	0	900
7026	Playground Equipment	0	0	0	
7028	Communication Equipment	0	0	0	
7030	Pumps and Motors	0	0	0	
7038	Microcomputer Equipment	0	3,500	3,378	2,000
7040	Books, Maps and Charts	0	0	0	
7088	Contra Account	0	0	0	
7099	Other Miscellaneous CIP	0	0	0	
	Total Capital Outlay	0	3,500	3,378	2,900
	Debt				
8001	Retirement of Bonds	0	0	0	
8002	Payment of Interest	0	0	0	
				0	
	Total Debt	0	0	0	0
	Non cash				
8102	Depreciation	0	0	0	

		1999	2000	2000	2001
		Actual $	Adopted $	Estimate $	Request $
	Total Non cash	0	0	0	0
9001	Other Contingency	25,000	485,244	468,260	500,244
	Total Other	25,000	485,244	468,260	500,244
	Grand Total	434,560	947,563	914,398	970,915

It is no wonder that managers work hard to expend every dollar approved in the budget before the budget year ends. This is the famous "end of the year spending" that seems to upset the public. It is absolutely necessary so the organization can meet its funding obligations in subsequent years. It is not necessary when the budgeting environment is enlightened and considers the needs of the organization's Programs and Core Activities.

A good budget process is another advantage of having a governing authority that is focused on the organization's vision and mission. Without that, an organization can easily begin a downward spiral of diminishing funds resulting in the loss or curtailment of Programs and Core Activities that are essential to the organization's vision and mission. The organization fails.

Chapter 19

Capital Projects

Some unmanageable organizations like Zoos and museums need to build things; buildings, exhibits, etc. Some managers feel they know enough about what they want that they start drawing up plans themselves. My advice; don't.

First, there is absolutely no substitute for professionals who can translate the vision and mission of the organization into brick and mortar.

Second, the organization must have a capital project Master Plan, again done by professionals who know what they are doing.

Master Planning professionals often serve the whole country and may not be located in your community. Governing authorities can be reluctant to approve or fund a study done by an "out of town" firm. One of the ways to sell this to a governing authority is to present a planning package that includes the "out of town" firm for Master Planning, individual project conceptual design and consultation then hire local firms for specific design, construction documents and project management. In some cities the City retains project management. In some organizations, the support group both funds and manages the project. The important idea is to spread some of the responsibility around to those groups that want some control, yet the organization's vision and mission are not compromised.

A capital project Master Plan must be done within the organization's vision and mission. Be sure that whatever firm you choose for this planning understands the vision and mission and agrees to work within that framework.

A capital project Master Plan must also be developed within the financial capabilities of the community to fund the projects and the organization's capability to operate them. I have seen many Master Plans that looked wonderful on paper but were way beyond the means of the organization to ever build or maintain. You must insist that an assessment of your community is done to determine the level of capital support that can be expected. In addition, you, along with the Master Planning firm must develop operating cost projections and revenue projections to ensure adequate operating support. These projections may necessitate increased subsidies from a governing authority. It would be great if you could get a commitment from the governing authority to provide the increased subsidy. Remember, though, unmanageable organizations often have governing authorities that change. The commitment you receive today may not be valid when the project is completed.

Include as many publics as possible in the capital Master Plan and individual capital projects. Just like the process for creating a vision and mission statement, including a variety of people in the project development will provide support for the project and a sense of ownership for those involved.

Certainly staff members need to be involved in capital project planning. It is not only important but also valuable to include staff that will be working in the building or exhibit in the planning process. If you are building a museum building, include the janitorial staff. You may be surprised what you can learn. Not only that, you may come away with a more efficient design for cleaning and other maintenance that will save the organization operating costs for the building.

Some organization must meet Federal, State and/or Local standards, not only for construction, but also for specific rules and regulations pertaining to what is located in the project. There may also be guidelines from your professional organization. As a manager, you need to know who will have input in your project and ensure the guidelines are met in the planning and construction phases.

As an example of these guidelines, let's say you are going to build a facility that houses orangutans. There will be local building codes to meet. There may be State regulations that govern disposal of waste, bedding, etc. There are Federal regulations governing most all aspects of housing orangutans from the size of the spaces to the types of material that can be used, etc. There are housing recommendations from the Zoological community that manages this species in Zoos. You must ensure all these requirements and recommendations are met and be sure the facility falls within the parameters of your organization's vision and mission.

Capital projects can be one of the most rewarding parts of being a manager. There is a lot of work too. Be prepared and remember to recognize all your supporters.

Chapter 20

Strategic Working

Creating a strategic plan usually results in a lot of paper that gets put on a shelf. Your day-to-day work continues as always. It's just that now you can say you have a vision and mission statement.

As a manager you must develop the ability to work strategically. That means you are working each day for the vision and mission. The decisions you make, the contacts you make, the reports you write, are all geared toward the vision, not for today. You are working in the future. It is not an easy thing to do and requires a lot of discipline. The most important thing is putting yourself in a mindset that allows the strategic plan to be your plan of action every day.

Your staff may not understand that you must distance yourself as much as practical from today's activities because you have to focus on the future of the organization. This is your primary job responsibility. I have sat in on many meetings where managers work on and determine details of the strategic plan but have no clue about how to "work the plan." After the plan is adopted, work continues as if nothing happened. If you don't know how to work the plan, don't even bother to go through the difficulty of creating the plan. Your organization may survive without a plan but the organization will not excel. You may survive also but you won't be a good manager. The unmanageable organization will remain so.

Here is the key question you must ask yourself and your staff each time a proposal is made or some decision must be made:

Does this proposal or decision fit or enhance our vision of the organization?

When I worked in a Zoo, it was not unusual for me to receive proposals that did not fit nor enhance the Zoo's vision or mission. I should not have even been given a proposal from Zoo staff that violated the Zoo's vision or mission. Those staff members either didn't buy in to the plan or did not know how to work the plan. An example of this, not an exact scenario but a combination of events, involves the acquisition of an animal. The vision and mission declare that animals will only be acquired if the Zoo has space that would be considered a "home" for the animal. Home, in this vision and mission, is based on the idea that it is hard to locate the line between nature and the "home space." The strategic plan also designates certain areas as themed areas. For example, an area is designated for Great Apes. So the proposal is made: There is room in the great ape visitor space that would accommodate several aquariums that could hold reptiles thus we should acquire the reptiles and put them in the available space. The organization's vision and mission are totally ignored in this proposal. The staff making this proposal and, if approved, the manager who approves it are not working the plan. If you see this incongruity in a Zoo or museum, you can be sure that the staff is not working the plan or there is no plan. These organizations are doomed to mediocrity.

In reality, every staff member should be working at least part of their time on the future. Each staff member will have a different level of involvement in the organization's plan for the future and none will have the involvement that you, as a manager, must have. It is important for you to ensure that all staff understands strategic working and knows that working the plan is expected of them. This can be accomplished by addressing this expectation in individual performance measures and performance evaluations.

In most unmanageable organizations the evidence of the lack of working the plan is easy to spot. There may be a vision and/or mission statement hanging on the wall but there is no attention to detail, no striving for excellence, no direction in day-to-day work activities and a number of mediocre staff. This is exactly the type of organization that politicians like and work hard to create and maintain. That is why government governing authorities create the most unmanageable organizations. Politicians don't really have a plan except for their own political futures and often feel threatened by excellence.

Chapter 21

Finally

Can you really manage an unmanageable organization? Probably not fully. However, you can create an environment in which the organization can thrive with real purpose by clearly identifying community needs and wants and having a vision and mission that are worthy. You can build a good team that will work hard for the organization's vision and mission. These can be done when the right governing authority is in place, when your support groups are truly supportive, when the community sees the organization as a valuable asset and the community leaders take responsibility for your organization's success. You and your organization must be knowledgeable and powerful enough to resist antagonists.

It can be done but it is work and there is a lot of luck involved. Remember, your competence, your knowledge and your skills may have little to do with the organization's success but those things are necessary for you to assist the organization. The organization's success is mostly based on your ability to recruit, train and educate others so they are competent, knowledgeable and have skills that will carry the organization forward regardless of who is the manager.

There are fewer individuals that retire from unmanageable organizations than individuals who change careers or just fade away. Some managers change with the governing authority. If you find yourself packing boxes rather than leading an important meeting, you must remember that it is not <u>your</u> failure. It is the failure of the organization that will not allow a good manager the freedom to facilitate success. It is their loss.

If you are a successful manager and someone exclaims, "This place is a zoo!" you can reply, "yes." Just like a Zoo, organized with a clear vision and mission and we are all working together.

About the Author

Mike LaRue began his career working organization as a summer zookeeper at the Topeka Zoological Park while earning a degree in Zoology at the University of Kansas. During more than 28 years at the Topeka Zoo, he worked his way up through all levels of the organization working his last 5 years as Zoo Director.

The author participated in numerous planning projects including strategic planning, master planning and capital improvement planning.

He implemented the Standards of Animal Care for the Topeka Zoo and set up performance measures for staff and subdivisions of the Zoo. He also put together and monitored budgets for most of his Zoo career.

The author has contributed to several books; *The Mother Earth Handbook* and *Przewalski's Horse: The History and Biology of an Endangered Species.* He has written numerous articles for a variety of publications.

0-595-23498-4

www.ingramcontent.com/pod-product-compliance
Lightning Source LLC
Chambersburg PA
CBHW031050180526
45163CB00002BA/766